"Sooner or Later"

The Stories and Adventures
of
The Odd Triple

By:
Bill Neel

Sooner or Later

Revised Printing,

Revised 2018
10 9 8 7 6 5 4 3 2

Published by: **The Odd Triple Press**
theoddtriplepress@gmail.com
Shirley, AR

Imprint of **Mixtus House Publishing**
Mixtushouse.com

ISBN (13) 978-1-71925879-1 (PB)
(10) 1719258791

Printed in the United States of America

Cast of Characters

The Odd Triple: *with Autographs*

BILL NEEL

ROCKY

PUFF

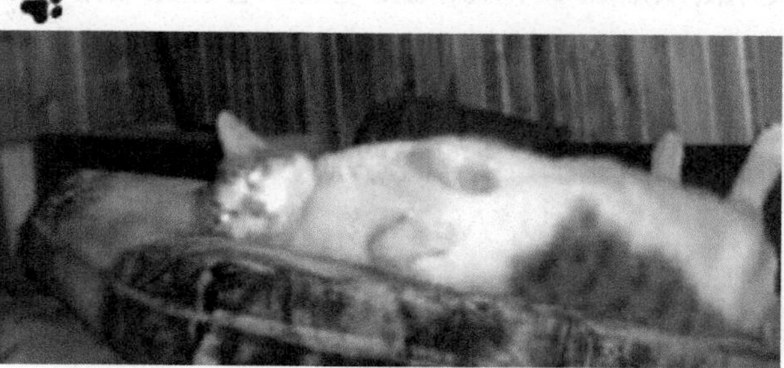

Table of Contents

Acknowledgments: VI

Forward: Sooner or Later – By: Bill Neel VII

Chapter 1: From Altus to Arkansas 1

Chapter 2: The Little Dipper 6

Chapter 3: Recycling, Dominos Pecans
and Family Days 13

Chapter 4: Honey 20

Chapter 5: Pair-Noid, Dirty Plates & Good Friends
"Uncle Bill's Funnies" 28

Chapter 6: Hard Times & the Creation of the
"One Carrot Onion Ring" 31

Chapter 7: Willy the Clown and the Shirley,
Arkansas Homecoming Parade 37

Chapter 8: *"Willy's Fish Tail"* and *"The Adventures of No Not Toe Basco"................... 40*

Chapter 9: *"Mower and Mower"* 46

Chapter 10: My Mom's Passing in Altus, Oklahoma 51

Chapter 11: *"Cars That Go Buy"* 55

Chapter 12: *"Rocky" & More of* Uncle Bill's Funnies" 65

Chapter 13: How I Got to Know Rocky the Wonder Dog 72

Chapter 14: Rocky the Wonder Dog With Too Much Time on Our Hands 88

Chapter 15: *"Toe Main Poyson"* and *"Small Houses"* 90

Chapter 16: Just Some Stunts for the Kids 94

Chapter 17: Willy the Clown - Palm Reading and *"Fun On the Coast"* 97

Chapter 18: *"Mall Tails"* 100

Chapter 19: *"Old School"* and *"Babysitting a G.P.S."* *103*

Chapter 20: *"Orkinsaw Anglish"* 106

Dedicate to Kenny Van Dalsem: a good friend of mine… *BN*

Forward
By: Bill Neel

I have wanted to start this book for several years, but never found the time. I am seventy seven at this time, and there is a little snow on the ground, and I am sitting in my living room here in North Arkansas with not much to do, so I thought this is a good time to start my book. Well, with me being 77, that was a good sign too. Hope all you folks like it.

I was born June 30, 1938 in Altus, Oklahoma to Delbert B and Annie L. Alderman, Neel. I know, the way I am even now, I gave my parents fits. Not real bad fits. All these many years I have never been arrested, never been in jail, and I also try to drive right with only a few traffic tickets as a kid. In 1942, February 28, I got to be big brother. I was 4. His name was Bobby K Neel.

I almost got ahead of myself. A couple of years before Bobby K was born, our family doctor told my parents I had a serious kidney problem. In a few months he told my parents I would not live to be 10 years old. I still remember going to the doctor at least once a week or more. My dad was real hurt, I could tell, and my mother was always in tears praying. I don't remember my age at the time, but they took me to Oklahoma City, OK. to some of the very best kidney doctors. I really didn't know I was about ready to leave this world. My mother praying had a big effect on what the doctors came back and told my mother and dad in the waiting room. They told them they could not find anything wrong with me. My parents were jumping with joy since they had thought that might be my first and last trip to Oklahoma City.

Bobby was with Cassey and Jedy Alderman, my mother's parents. He didn't have any kidney problems. I wanted to get Bobby's name at the first so people could see he had a good behavior record too.

I don't want you people to think I really spent the rest of my life in Altus. I didn't leave because I didn't like the city. My family did very well in Altus. As I was growing up, I like to fish and hunt. Now, are you getting the picture? I could see the lights of a town called Fredrick at night about 35 miles or so away. I also remember when I was seven and my brother was there, we had our tonsils taken out in the Altus Hospital (which, for many years has been the City Hall). My dad had an office in the City Hall.

He taught my brother and me how to fish and hunt. We would have to travel 50 miles or more to find the right fishing spots my dad knew about. My dad would put two or three dozen minnows in a minnow bucket. Then he would put aspirins in the bucket to temporarily put them out, so to speak. If he didn't do this, they would all be dead when we got to our favorite fishing spots. He would put the minnows in the running water and it would bring them back just like he had just bought them. He would cut willow limbs about as round as your finger and four to five foot in length, and put a line weight and hook. We would put the bait on the hook and put it in the "Creek" bank as far as we could, letting the hook and bait dangle in the water. The creeks were usually 20 foot wide more or less. We would come up the bank of the creek and find some sort of brush or small tree and tie a white rag to show where our poles were located. The rags would show up good at night also, when we would check the poles about every couple of hours. We had a boat, but this way was more fun. We had enough fish for ourselves and a lot to sell.

I know I said I like to hunt and fish. In Arkansas you can almost hunt and fish in your back yard. I'll get to it in just a minute about the "Land of Opportunity."

When I was a teenager along with my brother, Bob, my dad bought us a 410 shotgun. Back then they were made a lot different than they are now. Before my dad turned us out to hunt the big wild game (so to speak), he let us practice and get the feel of our gun.

My grandpa Neel had a big farm west of Martha, Oklahoma. How did he get this farm? He had one of these cute little telephone offices where one lady could connect all these people in Headrick, Oklahoma. That cute little phone company was really a going thing back in the 20's and 30's. This man saw my Grandpa Neel's big operation and traded his farm for my Grandpa's phone company. To make a long story short, my Grandpa Neel retired in the 1950's – and that same farm today is still producing. Wheat is one of the better crops.

I got side-tracked on the farm and telephone company. My brother and I would hunt near some hills on my Grandpa's place. I've got to tell you this one for sure. My brother Bob was not feeling too good and he stayed home with our mother in Altus, Ok. The only thing we had to hunt were Cottontail rabbits, Jack rabbits, and once in a while squirrels. My dad told me to go to the top of the hill. It was a pretty good climb. I thought, "Why is he sending me on top of this hill? I won't see any big wild game up here." He told me to get ready. He was at the bottom of the hill with a big stick. I thought "how crazy is it that he's going fishing and I am up here looking at empty space?" He told me to get my gun ready. There was brush at the bottom of the hill in some places, and he would stick the brush and the rabbit or rabbits would run up the hill. It was like shooting fish in a barrel. We would use the Jack rabbits for chili meat. We were overrun with rabbits. No limit. We would go almost every weekend and fish, camp out, cook on a campfire, and had a good time. We would leave on Friday evening and come home Sunday evening; and never had anyone to cause us problems. I wish I could go back to those days.

Oh yes, I almost forgot this: It's a little bit crazy. Just before I entered the fourth grade, my parents were teaching me ahead of the class. I was a real "whiz" at math. It wasn't that I was extra smart – like I said before, my parents were teaching me ahead of the class. I think the teacher should have stopped this. I could send all the kids in my room back to their desks. After a while I began to stutter real bad. I had no friends, and my parents could tell by the looks of my report card, they had done the wrong thing. I could not answer a phone or hold a conversation with very many people. My mother took me to our family doctor to find out if there was anything she could do to help me with my stuttering. It seemed to be getting worse. I was listening and I could not believe what he said. He told her my brain was going too fast for my mouth to deliver. All of you people out there who stutter are really pretty smart. I thought, "How in the world can I slow my brain to match my mouth." It is very hard to do, I find out. I stuttered for several years and seemed to be doing a little better. Keep reading my book and I will tell you how I quit stuttering completely. I had a real problem all the years I went to school. In middle school I got a paper route. It was a big route, and my brother Bobby helped me with half of it. Now this is hard to believe, but it was $1.02 a month. I passed a newspaper rack just recently and a single daily paper was $1.00. A lot of people complained when it went to 28 cents a week.

We could go to the bakery and get "real" donuts – 6 for 25 cents. Why so reasonable?

I was making $3.00 a day on my first job. I was working on a farm. You may think I didn't get to the Land of Opportunity by now, but just wait.

I met this young lady a while later and we got married. I got a job on the Fire Department and I was really happy, thinking this was my calling. We had a daughter and named her Daphne. If it hadn't been in the baby book, I would have spelled her name Daf-knee. Spelling was not one of my better choices in school. I'm glad I was never around the phone much at the fire Dept. It would have taken me a week to say "Fire Dept" on the phone. They sent me to all kinds of schools to learn more about my profession.

Well, my marriage did not work out too well, and we got a divorce. She took our daughter to California and I didn't think I would ever see my daughter again. I waited about 3 years or so before I tied the knot again. I dated several young ladies and I thought I might as well be a bachelor. Then I met this young lady. Her name is Alice. I never had cared for anyone so much. I thought that was in the movies. After a while we got married. I had quit the Fire Dept. and opened a couple of service stations. Service station business is not too bad of a business. {A service station owner in the late 1930's created the "Grapette Soda" in Camden, Ark., and it went worldwide.} I was doing okay with the service stations. We had a son. We named him Dennis. When Dennis was six months old I told Alice I'd like to make a change. Now you folks know by now how crazy I am. I told Alice I'm going to get the map of the U.S., and put it on my desk and get my ink pen, close my eyes and where ever the pen landed, we were moving there. It landed on Pine Bluff, Ark. We had never been to Ark., didn't have a job, no family, no place to stay, and a couple hundred dollars. This was 1968, about a week before my 30th birthday. I didn't want to ask my family for extra money. We didn't want anyone to know what we had done. We left Altus, Oklahoma on a Friday morning. Dennis was 6 months old. We packed what we could in this Ford station-wagon and started toward Oklahoma City, Oklahoma. It didn't soak in real good until I got a few miles on I-40 east out of Oklahoma City.

"*I'm glad I can look back on all of this and recall it just like it was happening today. Every time I get all stressed out from going out to see the rest of the world, I come back and write what I remember, and brother and sister, that is a lot, being 78. The ink is stronger than the stress.*"

Chapter One
"From Altus to Arkansas"

I didn't tell my wife, but I was almost ready to go back since my only son was 6 months old and I was starting my life all over again too.

A few miles before I got to the Arkansas line, I said to myself, "Lord, show me if I'm doing the right thing." As I went across the Arkansas line, there was a sign; "Land of Opportunity." That was what I really needed the way I was feeling. It's not that way anymore.

I wrote a letter to the Arkansas Governor in 1995. I did not hear from them as the sign changed to "the Natural State." Don't name a person "Bill" and the next day or two, name him "John" or a boy named "Susan." This is long before Martha Mitchell Freeway. (Before the "Land of Opportunity" it was "the Bear State").

We got to Pine Bluff on Saturday afternoon after we had a night at a campground Friday night. As we came into town on Dollarway Road, I looked and I thought, “this can't be all Pine Bluff has to offer.” As we kept driving, I noticed we were on the outskirts of Pine Bluff, Arkansas. I was just a big kid back then and I was ready to tackle anything to keep my family with their needs. I got a cheap motel room on Saturday evening. I got a Pine Bluff newspaper; and I looked for a cheap apartment. Nothing available. Next morning I got a Sunday Pine Bluff paper and found an apartment we <u>could afford</u>. Cheaper than the motel. As you remember, anything would look good when you don't have a job, don't know anyone, and have a 6 month old boy and his parents to feed. I kept thinking about the welcome sign on I-40. “<u>Land of Opportunity.</u>” This is what kept me going.

Back before I came to Arkansas, I was in the Army. We didn't back down after President John F. Kennedy sent us to Fort Stewart, Georgia to take care of business. This was during the Cuban Missile Crisis.

I left the apartment early Monday morning not knowing what to expect. I checked several service stations and found no kind of employment. I had worked on waterworks for my dad, so I checked that and found the city had no control of that system. To get a job on the city, they said I would have to talk to the mayor. I'm thinking, “my first day in town, and I'm going to ask the mayor for a job.” I'm sure glad I was able to speak better and not stutter a lot. To find work to support my family, I would have to talk to the mayor for two weeks trying to explain why I was in his office. I guess if he had hired me, I would have worked the first year without a vacation because I took up 2 weeks of his time trying to get a job. Ha Ha! I guess, in a way I got lucky when he told me he didn't have anything. Well, I didn't stutter either, but read on and you will see why I worded this so crazy. He went to his drapes and opened them and told me to check the employment office. It was near lunch time. I looked out the window and saw Gibsons Discount Store. I had never done any work of this kind before.

I decided to check Gibsons first and if no employment was there, then I would go to the employment office. I got to Gibsons right at 12 noon. I asked the clerk in the front to see the manager about a job. She said he was going out the front door and to check with him before he left. I managed to get to talk to him just before he left for lunch. I asked him if he had any openings. I nearly fell over by what he said. He said, "The Lord must have sent you. One of our employees broke in the store during the weekend and we need someone. Can you be at work at 1 pm?" Gosh, I had less than an hour to go tell my wife and get a snack. I was so happy I had found a job so quick.

As time passed, we had met a lot of new friends. I was really Home Sick and also my wife had it bad too. There are no doctors that can help you. We made every excuse to go back to see our family. We let our families know where we were just a few days after we got settled. They couldn't believe we had done this with a small child.

As time went by, I was in charge of the automotive dept. in Gibsons. I kept looking for greener grass. I got a job as assistant manager of a dry goods store. I worked selling appliances on my next job, and then a vending company. I still think about the Welcome Sign as I drove into Arkansas – "Land of Opportunity."

"I thought, I know the Lord put that sign before me for some reason. I will never give up. I worked for this store that got to be real popular doing openings as "Willy the Clown." This store, Wal-Mart, only had a few stores at this time. I covered 16 states doing openings – not only for that store but several other big stores.

I was really happy; but it was taking a toll on my family. I had 3 sons and was not home real often. I couldn't support my family on lower wages. I saw what was happening and I couldn't get out. I tried once to sell furniture. At least I could stay at home. I got to be Manager of one of their stores; but then they went out of business. Well, here I am, back where I started. We didn't stay together long. I had been "Willy the Clown" for so long, it was like another person. I was entirely a different person when I put on my makeup, suit and clown shoes. I knew Cactus Vic with Wonder Bread real well.

My entire life, I had good parents; and I'm not saying I am perfect, but you can run a check on me from the time I first went to school (6) until now at this writing. I will be 78 this last day of June 2016; and you will not find anything wrong I have ever done to be in any kind of trouble with the law of any kind except a few speeding tickets when I was a kid.

One other thing I can also say. Whenever I put Willy the Clown away in his briefcase every day, nobody, yes nobody ever checked my case to see if I had put something in it. Only the manager knew who I was. I would have gladly let anyone in the store I happened to be in, look inside of my briefcase at any time they wanted to check it. I have never taken anything that wasn't mine. I have no trouble going to sleep at night.

As you remember at the very first of this book how my Dad took me fishing and hunting; all of a sudden, I had no family in Arkansas. Alice and I were now single parents; and I guess it was a lot of doing Willy the Clown. I was doing ok with this and I thought I had to do this because I wanted what was best for my family. I put Willy away for a long time.

Just before I became single, I moved to Coy, Ark. For a short while. I left Coy and went to England, Arkansas. It seemed as I was starting over again. I didn't know anyone in town. I found a place to live. I was employed for a while at the Department of Correction at Tucker. I was in the first class of the Academy for the Department that was located in the West Pine Bluff area.

"I may give out but never give up."

Bill Neel

Chapter Two
"The Little Dipper"

I did very well in England; and also started an ice cream parlor similar to Baskin Robins. I called it the "Little Dipper." I did a lot of work on it and made it look real sharp.

In 1973 they were filming a movie in the England, Ark. area called "White Lightning" starring Burt Reynolds. This began at the Dept. of Correction – Tucker Unit, Tucker Arkansas. Tucker is about 10 or 15 miles south of England, Ark. Burt Reynolds had escaped from the Tucker Unit. He had a car shortly thereafter, and soon the England Ark. Police were waiting for him. As he got into England, Ark., he took a left, which took him downtown. Just before he got to the traffic light to go right to Little Rock, Ark., the police were right behind him and Burt Reynold's car crashed near the Bank of England. He left his car, trying to get away, and ran across the street to this building. For a brief moment. A few years after this movie was made, the "Little Dipper Ice Cream Parlor started in the same building. After the Little Dipper was open for a while, people began to tell me, Burt Reynolds had been in the "Little Dipper." What will I do next??

Before I opened the Little Dipper Ice Cream Parlor, I asked some of the people in England, Ark., what would be a good business for this great little city. I had planned to try something. I don't like working for the other fellow. I talked to several people who had been there for many years. Most all of them asked for a regular Ice Cream Parlor. They had a small place in town selling fast food and had only vanilla and chocolate hand-dipped.

As I told you folks before how crazy Uncle Bill is. I went to Searcy Ark. To talk to Mr. Yarnell. He said, "Mr. Neel, I've seen a lot of Ice Cream Parlors fold." He was real nice trying to tell me I might try another line of work so to speak. This was in the late 70's.

"Well, if at first you don't suck seed, suck and suck till you do suck seed." {*Willy the Clown* advice}

I knew some people in Pine Bluff, Ark., who sold ice cream and other dairy products. I talked to them and they said "get you a nice building and we will bring the freezers and ice cream." They had as many flavors as the big stores where I took lessons on dipping ice cream. I sold not only ice cream, but banana splits, milk shakes, hot fudge sundaes and much more. It was real cute when these couple of kids whose parents had the other ice cream (fast food) would buy ice cream from me. As it went on, we got a cotton candy machine – no waiting for fairs and carnivals.

I also had a Donut Shop in the front part of the Little Dipper. I had a friend in Little Rock, Arkansas who owned a <u>Major Name Donut Shop</u>. I would make a trip to Little Rock every morning early; real, real early and pick up all kinds or pastries. What we didn't sell we donated to retirement homes and any other people we could help. We had a special container just for this purpose in the back of my pickup truck. There were several churches in the England Arkansas area that would bring their pastry list on Saturday afternoon; I would see that they had everything on their list, plus what we sold in the Little Dipper. I didn't do this for money since everyone needs beans, taters, and turnip greens. I enjoy helping people. I told you folks before that I had a bigger family in England Arkansas than anyone. Yes, I might have moved from England Arkansas, but every day I get a call from England Arkansas. I will never forget what that little city did for me.

One other thing about the Little Dipper; In the Southwest part of Oklahoma we had these Special Ice Drink Machines; I will not put a name on these. They were a big treat for the kids and also adults. Since I had moved to Arkansas I had never seen one. At this time I had been in Arkansas several years. I kept telling my employees in the Little Dipper that this would make my Bucket List complete. One night as I was closing the Little Dipper I saw this pickup going by. It had a name on the door advertising the machine I wanted. I was saved by the traffic light in England. Just as he got to it, it turned red and stopped him. I'm thinking: Oh No! Is he from Roswell too! I got to talking to him and in a couple of weeks I had a machine.

…Just got to thinking; Maybe I'm from Roswell too. Ha-Ha! *Uncle Bill 2017*

I quit the Dept. of Corrections and put all my time into the Little Dipper. I had a lady and her daughter helping me. It really was these two that really made it busy. I had a friend at Pine Bluff who had cigarette machines. He asked if he could put one in the Little Dipper. I didn't make much with it, but people were using it. One day when my friend came to check the cigarette machine, he told me he knew these people in Pine Bluff who had pinball machines, pool tables and much more. I told my friend I'd like to talk to these people. I had a large ice cream parlor, and could put a pinball machine in an out-of-the-way place so it didn't interrupt my ice-cream parlor. The kids from miles around had not much to do, so they came to see (Uncle Bill). Adults did too. The pinball machine, for my part, was paying my electric bill. I was so busy, I had them bring another machine. Soon it was paying my rent. I would go to Little Rock to the big ice cream parlors and get an ice cream cone, sit back and take lessons.

There was this businessman in England, Ark. Who had one of the "Big Name" (I'll call it that) ice cream parlors in Little Rock, Ark., and one in Hot Springs. I knew him pretty good.

All of a sudden, everyone in England knew Uncle Bill. I think this man saw what he and others overlooked. Then, Olan Mills Photographers wanted to rent a space in the Little Dipper for one day. They would come back in a few days with the customers' photos. They could not believe the traffic that was coming in for ice cream and photo shoots. They changed that one day into three days. They became regular renters, so to speak. I could hardly believe this was happening.

Awhile later these people came by from the eastern part of Ark. (Brinkley area) and liked my ideas I had for the Little Dipper; and asked me if I had planned to franchise it. I thought, "Bill, now remember the welcome sign." Arkansas is the "Land of Opportunity."

I really had the Little Dipper – dipping so to speak. One day the man with the amusement machines asked me if I wanted to open a "Game

Room." He really said "Pool Hall" - but my words sound better. I knew how to handle people without too much trouble since I worked at the Dept. of Correction for a while at the Tucker Unit. I told these people I had hardly ever been in a Game Room – and now I have a Game Room. I was extra busy with that in no time. It was like Santa had come to town. The game room was located on the west side of the Square. I could look out the big window of the Game Room and I had a bird's eye view of the Little Dipper. It looked like I missed my spot on the map when I was looking for somewhere to call home. The Lord guided me to this small town south of Little Rock, Ark. I was doing the same as these big stores.

To be successful in business or anything, you have to keep your customer happy. Also, have products he or she doesn't have to travel 50 to 75 miles more or less. They can purchase within a few blocks. Give it some thought before jumping in. If you see many many fast food places or beauty shops, or any other I haven't mentioned – that is a red flag. You can be anywhere and succeed. Remember at the beginning of this book how I started. I don't recommend you do what I did. That was 1968. This is a different world. We didn't have all the modern technology. If you did that today and you were in a driverless car, it would get a few miles out of town and come back home on its own. Ha Ha!

I want to thank you people in England, Ark. Customers came from all over Jefferson County, Southern Loanoke County – people from Little Rock bringing pecans – people from Brinkley, Ark. I tried to help as many people as I could. I still take the England Democrat Newspaper. Jerry Jackson and the late Ben Hicks were also a big blessing. I will never forget you people in England, Arkansas!

The bus station was next to the game room. One hot day in July, the bus left – going east and had a major motor problem with a bus load of people in front of the Little Dipper. What were these people to do on a hot day? ...I had nothing to do with that problem! *BN*

The bricks on this home were once the bricks on the Little Dipper Ice Cream Parlor. Fire took the Little Dipper away. Gone, but not forgotten. A lot of people would have given up. Not Uncle Bill. It was his health that slowed him down.

Why Oh Why did they take the Land of Opportunity away! *BN*

In the first part of the 80s, just before I was employed at the Department of Corrections at Tucker Arkansas, I went to an employment agency in Pine Bluff where I was to start as a Sales Representative for a Pharmaceutical Company. They asked me if I had any college. I told them no. They told me to show up anyhow. I tried to save my family and did not take this job. Besides, I would be on the road some of the time.

I was so mixed up and about to lose my family… I still did real well with the Little Dipper, Neel's Recycling, Neel's Pecans and Produce Company. It was meant for me to take this route instead of the other job.

Chapter Three
Recycling, Dominos, Pecans & Family Days

I had in the past performed as Willy the Clown. I noticed over the past few years, I was performing Willy the Clown in places with 250 on the population sign.

You would see many many school busses around the school. The people who had these big stores (except for one) were overlooking people in the country. When anything big was going on, I had never seen so many people in my life. When they first sent me to a small town like I just mentioned, I thought it would be a waste of time to put Willy to work. I found out real quick, "you can't judge a book by its cover."

I always tried to do my makeup and have everything right. It would take about a couple of hours to get ready. It seemed the smaller towns were eager to see things like this. This goes to show the world that it's ok to take business into small towns. They spend money too. In a few months I bought a building and a Game Room. As you remember, I came to England, Ark. Hitchhiking, and with very little money. I gave almost everything I had to Alice and my three boys. She took them to Roswell, New Mexico. We had been divorced for a while!

I said I had quit stuttering and would tell everyone how I quit. I think the love I had for Alice and the boys helped me a lot. Once in a great while, I find myself starting to stutter again. I'm doing ok with it.

After a period of time, Bill Neel Jr. moved to San Antonio, Texas with his mother. Just before the boys first moved to Roswell, New Mexico, I would take each one to have a good time on the weekends. My boys were Dennis, Danny and Billy Jr. A short time before my family moved to Roswell, New Mexico, Dennis, my oldest son was a junior in High School. He got his first job as a disc jockey for the small radio station on the west side of England on Clear Lake Road. I won't put his boss's name in this. He is a real busy TV person – even as I speak in 2016. One day I took Dennis to his work and Dennis knew how to close the station. It didn't stay on the air real late. I went back to take him home and he started showing me how to start turning different things off as the broadcast day was over. Then he said, "Dad, I've got to use the restroom." Now I can handle things of almost any kind, but you don't go into the first grade and the next day you get your High School diploma. I was a little shook up, and didn't want the people in Little Rock or other cities to get excited like "the British are coming!"

I'll tell a cute one about Billy Jr. since I'm on this funny stuff. By the way, Dennis got out in the nick of time.

I took the boys camping. We needed some twigs and larger wood to start our campfire. Dennis and Danny were somewhat older than Billy. I told them to get some twigs to help start the fire much better. Dennis went one way. Danny went another. Little Billy would take on any kind of project - no matter what it might be. Billy learned a real valuable lesson with this project. It's best to read or ask questions before you try to put anything together! Dennis and Danny came back with a lot of twigs. Billy did not see what they were doing. It was a good while and Billy walked up to me and said, "Dad, what is a twig?" While I am writing this, a little tear came into my eyes. Right now Billy is in his early 40's, and I still poke him every now and then about the twigs. I could write things like this I still remember how the boys were active. Many people don't have this in their lives. I am very blessed. We all wish things were different, but some-where down the road, you will see a reason for everything happening like it was meant to be. All three of my sons are very successful. I am so proud of them.

Now back to England, Ark. Now you are thinking; 'What else could Bill have in England?' It really was little Billy's idea, and I took his idea and ran with it, so to speak. I had Billy for the weekend. He said, "Dad, let's try something different this weekend. I want to walk the country roads and pick up aluminum cans. This was something new back then. At times they were paying 35 to 40 cents a pound. We also got some good exercise. It takes 24 cans to make a pound. We would walk a mile

section. We were doing fair. I told Billy Jr. I was going to Little Rock and check with Reynolds Aluminum Company to set us up to buy cans and all other grades of aluminum. I learned all of the grades of metal so I could pay the customer a little more for better grades of aluminum. Reynolds would send an 18 wheeler to my place in England, Ark. Every other week. Also, a can crusher that blows cans in the 18 wheeler. As time went by, the biggest metal Recycler in Arkansas came by several times trying to get me to deal with them. They had Alcoa Aluminum. I finally decided that looked like the best way to go. With them, I could not only deal in aluminum products; I could deal in copper, brass, stainless steel and other metals. After a short time, I went to Little Rock and they taught me the different grades of copper, brass and many more metals.

Now, can you folks wonder why I got upset because they took away the "Land of Opportunity?"

RECEIVE DONATION — Members of Mrs. Hill's Resource Cla
receive a donation from Bill Neel. The money will be used to bu
calculators to help the students with their math skills.

Resource Class collecting cans

use the income from the sale of
cans to finance trips and for vario
projects.

Class members collect cans du

I had no help when I first come over to the Land of Opportunity. Dennis was born in Altus, Oklahoma – and Danny and Billy were born in Pine Bluff. I hear a lot of people saying they don't like Pine Bluff. I know of two people who started their business there and did extremely well. I worked in the same business with one and the other, I shopped at his Mexican Restaurant, and later on he had Peanut Oil Fried Chicken. Now it seems like burger and fries are better. Nothing comes to us over night. You have to keep going, and not let anyone tell you it won't make it. (No need to wear a watch).

After the scrap metals got real busy, people coming by would ask me if later on I might buy pecans in the fall. I told people they could take their pecans to George just down the street from me. I finally closed the Game Room. I put some of the silver beauty rings and hub caps on the wall; and not only car dealers, but just everyday folks were shopping in the front of my building.

I was dealing with the City of England on all of their scrap metals and also this big electric company would give their employees scrap pieces of copper wire in large drums. I told them how to separate their copper and could receive more money for it. Later I opened a small scrap yard in Stuttgart, Ark. It was hard to find the right help and I was so busy on other projects, I finally closed the scrap yard in Stuttgart.

One day these older fellows came by and said they had no place to play dominoes. I had plenty of room at the front of my building; and I told them to bring their tables and chairs and "do your thing." I had played dominoes since I was a kid with my Mom and Dad. Bobby and friends would play. My Mom could beat everyone back then. They kept wanting me to take money for this. I told them "no." What I really wanted was someone to let me play dominoes and relax when I got older. I finally told them if you want to pay – what about each of you pay 3.00 a month? It was so cute to see their faces. It was like we know we are paying our way and they seemed to feel better about it. Now, here we go again. After a period of time, one of the domino players came to me and asked me if I wanted to buy pecans. He was getting on in age and he said he couldn't take care of it any longer. He gave me the phone number to talk to the people to develop a market for the pecans.

Oh, I still remember I-40 all right. I still remember these people on TV many years back telling Elvis Presley he wasn't good enough for their show. Sometime later, the man who said this to Presley, said anyone can be on my show.

Back to the Pecan Company. Really, we called it all "Neel's Recycling Co." It was really busy too since it was connected with the scrap metals.

The Lord has blessed me so much. Most of the people give their money away after they have passed away. Not everyone is the same. They say everyone has a twin. I would have hired him back then if he had dropped by to see me. (Ha ha). I am not a rich person. I never wanted to be a rich person. Just to get by and not let too much bother you. With the Recycling business and the Pecan Company, every week I would pick out customers no matter if they brought me 5 pounds or an 18 wheeler load of metal or pecans and take them out to dinner. I found a lot of people in extra bad shape that I helped as much as I could.

I want to tell this before I go to the Produce Company. One year, just before Thanksgiving, I would tell my customers to put their name in a big box for a Thanksgiving Dinner. No, not a fast-food place. People need to fix their own meals like they once did. It seems to taste better. I picked out this family's name out of the box and to start off, I gave her the turkey. She was a young lady (and I knew these people) – {no, I didn't cheat}. A few days later, this family came in to tell me they enjoyed their meal; and she told me (no joke) that she could hardly get the turkey out of the oven. It's things like that, that makes me glad.

I came to the "Land of Opportunity." I have been in Arkansas for 48 years.

After I retired, I was the second person to manage the Clinton Recycling Center way back. I knew Mr. and Mrs. Hippie real well. She always said she was "Mrs. Hippie" the state. I miss them even today.

Chapter Four
"Honey"

Now, for my last business before I moved to the Shirley, Ark., area. This all went together pretty much. By this time, I had lost the Little Dipper to a fire which took the entire block. It sat in the middle of the block. They said the Little Dipper was the last to go. I was in Altus, Oklahoma visiting my mother when I got the call. It was like losing a member of the family. When I got back to England, I tried to find the right location I needed. I tried once or twice, and it just didn't like its new home each time. <u>I can always look at the good side for the Little Dipper. This is where everything started for me. I remember talking to this man who was in the ice-cream business. He told me the Little Dipper would never make it.</u>

If anyone comes to me with all kinds of crazy ideas, I will always listen and never downgrade what they have to offer – unless it would be something illegal. I was telling this man today, I live in a little cabin. I drive a 1994 Ford pickup. I've had all this for years and years, and I try to be happy. A big extra nice home will burn same as a cabin. The Rolls Royce will fall apart just like my pickup; and the land you have at the very last looks just like everyone's. I'm not saying I want people to smile and be happy when they walk by. There would be less people at the doctor's office.

Sorry I got side-tracked. Now – Neel's Produce Co. The company who bought the pecans also had watermelons, pumpkins, potatoes, and onions. I was ok with this produce. It had a long long shelf life. I did real good with this business. Oh yes, we also had a couple of machines to crack pecans.

I retired in 1995 and the large Recycling Company in Little Rock rented Neel's Recycling from me for a while. Now I'm not bragging – just facts: After a while it was like, 'where's "Mr. B"? Along with the scrap metals, the big recycling company also was buying pecans. They told me they had never seen such a business develop in such a short time. This company started many many years ago buying furs. So you can see what you can do if you don't give up when you have a lot of bad days in a row. They finally left England, Ark. And several more people tried it. As far as I know, there is no recycling company in England, Ark. As of this writing – May – 2016. There are people still buying pecans (puh-cons) in the fall. I can never thank these two companies enough for helping me in the recycling and pecan business. I'll have to admit – at times I wanted to quit. Being in a state without family close by, it's real easy to have thoughts of leaving and your nearest family is about 1,000 miles away, give or take. I have always been a family person. I know the outside of me has changed, but my heart for my family will never change. It seems even now (or let's say for a long time) I wanted to move near San Antonio, Texas. My youngest son and his wife are realtors and would have no problem helping me.

About 6 or 8 months ago, I was almost ready to go. I have some friends who live in the Fairfield Bay area who give me newspapers and cardboard to help me start my fires in the large wood heater I have. I started home and the wind was blowing pretty much. When I load anything in my truck, I try to see that everything is packed right; and when I arrive at my destination, everything is still there. I always try to keep an eye on my outside mirror. I had gone a mile or so and just a small amount flew from my truck into a ditch. I found a place to turn around. I pulled off the highway to a safe place and picked up my few pieces of paper. Like I say, I was ready to leave this state and go to Texas. It was meant for this paper to fly out at this spot. As I started to get in my truck, I saw this piece of Styrofoam partly covered in leaves. I was going to leave it laying there. As I picked it up, I could not believe what I saw. It was not perfect, but it looked like the State of Arkansas, Land of Opportunity. The Lord sent me here in 1968 and I guess that was saying "don't leave just yet – You still have some work to do.

Even before this, a friend asked me if I wanted to sell raw honey. I told him I'd think about it. I had been retired for a while, and I was sitting outside in my lawn chair, counting cars. I think maybe one or two got by me because of the trees. At that time, I might see a couple of cars in 6 months or so. I finally told my friend, "I'll come out of retirement and try it." I got a few jars of honey and I started "Uncle Bill's Honey. The label on the honey is really the name of the company. I painted a sign, and away I went. I tried a couple of locations, and couldn't get people to even ask for the price.

Like I said - "Don't ever give up or let someone tell you it won't make it." I finally found the third spot. They always say the 3rd time is the charm.

I got to set up at this location, and it started out like the other two locations I had to fix the problem Mr. B had. (No, he had quit stuttering long ago). Along with everything else I have done, I also had a few bee hives. My Grandfather Neel had bee hives in the 1920's. So, you can see by this, I really knew something about what I'm doing. Now, what was wrong? It was my sign. I painted the letters on that with a big paint brush. The sign had – "Honey for Sale." If your bee hives are 25 miles, give or take, from your honey sales, you can put "Local Honey" on your sign. It is local honey - since it's bottled just north of Shirley, Ark. I am now doing ok with this after they taste the honey.

I have people ask me a lot of questions about my product. I would not sell any kind of product that I wouldn't use myself. Here are a couple of questions. 'Do you live in Clinton?' Well, I guess that makes Fairfield Bay look pretty good. Like, if I am going to get rich on this honey business, why would I leave Highway 65 and go to Dave Creek Parkway? Just one more for you all. I had a customer ask me if I had 100% clover honey. I'm not a dishonest person. I would never say I had any sort of honey to get a customer. I could stick a label over the one on the bottle. I told them to taste the honey. They drove off. That didn't bother me one bit. I have a saying that "having friends is like having a garden! Once you get rid of your weeds, you've got a pretty good crop."

The way I believe about any 100% flavor in the honey you buy. The bee-keeper would have to have caged bees – which I have never seen before. If the world was covered in clover, there would be a few wild flowers here and there. *BN*

'You can't tell your bees not to get the wild flower pollen and get only the clover pollen.'

Ok folks, I have another project going. Awhile back I noticed this small advertisement on TV showing this young man riding his bicycle, throwing newspapers. As time passed, he donated the bike to Goodwill; and soon a little boy saw the bike, and his parents got it for him. The bike was not new, but in the little boy's eyes it was new to him. I'm not leaving out the little girls. I don't have room to store these, and people would have a hard time getting here. Not only should Foster children have bikes and other things – the families who rarely ask for anything could use a bike or two for their children since a lot of people working are having a hard time. You can usually tell who these people are. I was at one time having some trouble keeping my family with their needs. I didn't want to ask for help. There are a lot of families out there (young and old) right now are in trouble. I have found some of them. I'll tell you about mine. After that happened, things began to get better for me. I will never forget it as long as I live. I was still married to Alice, and we were still living in Pine Bluff Ark. I had a pretty good job. There were a lot of things I did without. I love my family very much. My station-wagon was not in real good shape. I would walk to work and most of the time I would take a little snack for lunch. Once in a great while, I would walk home for lunch, even if I only got to spend a few minutes. One day this pastor was visiting my home during the few minutes I was going to be there. I had my legs crossed in this chair while I was talking to him. I didn't do this for him to notice my shoes. He asked me what size shoes I wore. I told him, and he said, "I just bought these shoes a few days back, and I want to trade my shoes for yours." They were the same size I wear. I was never so "touched" in my life. I am a soft-hearted person, and a little tear came in my eye. I didn't really want to do that. I had never been in real bad shape before. I can't help everyone who asks. I try my best to help all I can. I can truthfully say this and everyone knows I'm right. There are a lot of real wealthy people out there and a short distance away people are hungry. Remember about the little used bicycles. Remember about a pair of shoes you have in the closet. You don't have to give money. I have a little granddaughter in another state. I was making a mistake with her. Don't send her money for important days. If nothing else; send her a picture of you, your dog and cat. Sometimes as much trouble that's in the land, maybe that's all you can do. I'm not trying to change you people. I'm just telling you what is in my heart and the way I feel. Most people do ok a couple of days a week and after that, you are back in your little world. The other day I saw this young lady taking a smoke break. I told her I smoked real much when I was in the service. I told her I haven't smoked in about 25 years. How did I quit? My kidneys failed me in 1995, and I looked like a skeleton. They called my family in. I stayed at the VA for several weeks – part of it was in ICU. I was only to live to be about 10 years old at first. Look at me now. Later I saw the same young lady with these other people on smoke break. I don't know this young lady. She was the only one in the crowd that would listen to me. I walked by and she said, "Mister, I'm trying to do what you told all of us sitting here to do. She is now taking some sort of medicine to help her gradually quit smoking. I tell people things and if they don't want to listen, that's ok. I've tried. I'll say this if you are on something. That is not good for your body. Don't wait until you look the way I did in the V.A. It's best never to start any kind of habit and donate what you are spending for something you don't need, and help someone who is really in need.

There is a lot more I'd like to write. Some of it I wouldn't put on paper. No, it's not vulgar words. It's something we all see every day and we do nothing about it. *Bill Neel 5-11-2016*

When I was in the fourth or fifth grade in school, we would take small nap breaks. Everyone but Bill Neel would take a little nap every day. I would have my pen and paper, drawing store fronts like – "Bill's Hardware," Bill's Grocery," and so on. All the kids laughed at me. It is really something how the Lord works. I had all kinds of ideas in Altus, Okla., but nothing seemed to go right. I did not know about the sign on I-40 when I left with my family. I try to stay by myself as much as I can. To tell you the truth, I am glad I am here and I will never move away. Maybe visit – but not move.

Oh yes, I was talking about small towns people we're overlooking. Now on the TV news is a young man in Romance, Ark. who is the youngest Blacksmith around, making knives and rifles; and is so busy he is now known nationwide on a special channel on TV that features these sort of projects. He is not taking orders at this time. He is so busy. He was on channel 11 News showing his operation. I told you people many years ago – “don't over-look the small towns, no matter where they are.” *Bill Neel*

I just feel like saying this. I have a few people almost every day tell me about all of my faults. No, not my honey customers. They are glad I'm there. It would be better for all if they would spend that time they use, talking nice to their friends and neighbors.

“I can make earplugs from beeswax.” *Bill Neel*

Chapter Five

Pair-Noid, Dirty Plates & Good Friends
* Uncle Bill's Funnies *

I'm not moving away – only to visit. I had planned to go to San Antonio, Texas to see Billy Jr. and his family. Number one on the list is Kylee, Billy's new daughter. I got side-tracked just before my birthday when I got a letter. The VA wanted me in for a checkup in Little Rock, Ark. I plan on going to see Billy, Pam and Kylee in the fall and take my very first train adventure. I plan on staying a week or two and going back to the dome and watching a football game. The last time I went, I sat on the 50 yard line.

"If what you have read in the last few pages is boring and you are still stressed out, watch Green Acres every morning."

Bill Neel

"No, I'm not rich. A lot of donations I made never got to the right people. I know this for a fact."

Bill Neel - Willy the Clown

“Uncle Bill's Funnies”

I do not copy from anyone. It just comes to me.

My grandson stayed with me here on the 5 – AKERS for a while. I told him if he wanted to stay, he would have to help grandpa do chores. I was in my late 60's and he was a late teenager. I told him if he wanted beans, taters and turnip greens, he would have to break his habit of playing games on my TV everyday while grandpa was toiling or mostly boiling in the hot sun and shade. I was reading my horror-scope book; and it was saying I could take a lot of punishment for something I believe in. Well, I guess I will have to write a new horror-scope book. I threw that one away. I had all I could take, and I was ready to take care of business. I was in the army. He was always talking about Pair-Noid!! I asked him if he knew what that word mint. He was trying to tell me and I stopped him. I knew he had never looked at my “Orkinsaw Dictionary.” I told him, Pair Noid means two Noids. He asked me “What's a Noid?” I said, “Grandpa!!” I gave him a few “going away” parties. The last party must have stuck. I haven't seen him for a while. I love my family. I'm not going to baby sit into their teenage years. Read my book when I came to the Land of Opportunity. I got a job and so can you. I still get a-Noid every now and then; but not by my grandson.

Bill Neel 8-30-2016

"Having Good Friends"

Bill Neel, 8-30-2016

I have found that having good friends is like having a garden. Once you rid yourself of weeds, you have a real good crop.

P.S. That's a good steady job, too. Might ought to wear gloves.

I left my little funny before this one. I forgot to tell you why my grandson left on the last party. As you remember, he did not overdo himself working. He was always in good shape when I gave him spending money or his meals. Well, about a week before the last "Going Away Party", I happen to think how bad it was years back. When I was a kid, it was so bad they would put a dirty plate on the table and I would think I had already ate. Well, I guess it works. I got me a job and my grandson is probably still looking at dirty plates if he is strong enough. Moral of this story is "Dirty plates are still dirty no matter whose table they are on." *Bill Neel 8-30-2016*

"Orkansaw Anglish:"

Brief-case – Something to carry underwear in.

Chapter Six

"Hard Times and the Creation of the One Carrot Onion Ring"

This has to do with Willy the Clown. He was always looking for ways to M-press his little friends. Clowns do not wear jewelry, and Willy the Clown fixed that. People laughed at me. Well, I would laugh harder when I tickled my ribs.

(I am serious). People, as of today that know me out of costume for years, still really don't know me. Some of the people I know can't believe all the things I have done since I came to Arkansas, "Land of Opportunity."

I would say that some of the people think I came from Roswell, New Mexico, and I crawled from the wreckage unseen and made my way to Altus, Oklahoma. It was a tough trip. I broke my bottle several times. When I got to Altus, Okla., I found a big cardboard box. I hopped in, pushed the doorbell and started to scream. Gosh, this is starting to sound like my grandson's story. Did I catch something from him??? The couple came to the door and the lady told her husband to rush and wash the dirty dishes and she would fix me some- thing to eat. She checked me over and she told her husband this kid has survived on Cactus Juice and Cactus Candy forever. She fixed a big meal and she always had an onion. I took a big bite of onion. I thought it was more cactus so to speak. I began to have all kinds of fits. My Dad was like Bill Neel. He could fix anything – (but cactus). He said, "Give the kid more onion. If a little does a little good, a whole lot will do a whole lot'ta good." Before I could get all those onions down, my mother said, "Run to my purse and get this kid a breath mint." Do you know when he got back with my breath mint, it was no time until I noticed the dirty plate. I had already eaten. Can you imagine what it would cost today for a house call??? I still had the craving for onions, but could not eat them. Keep reading, and you will see how I fixed that.

P.S. My ex-wife left England, Ar. She took the boys to Roswell, New Mexico. I made one trip to see them before she moved again. *Bill Neel 8-30-2016*

Now the One Carrot Onion Ring for sure!

"The One Carrot Onion Ring"

I wish I had come up with this idea before I retired *Willy the Clown*. I got to use my idea a few times. I have pictures and several "One Carrot Onion Rings" to this day. I'm not going to tell everything about the ring. I might get a "Colly-flower-ear." *BN*

I know Dale and Kay Shull who live in the Fairfield Bay, Ark. Area. Mrs. Shull and a few more ladies at the Indian Rock Village Retirement Home were entertaining residents at the home, and also other homes and different projects as clowns. The Shulls knew I had performed as Willy the Clown for a good while, and almost knew what I was doing. The reason I put it that way is you can learn something new every day. I went to visit their Clown Group. Yes, at the time, I thought I knew everything. Oh, how wrong could I have been? I went to help these ladies to show them some of the things I did, such as makeup, and all kinds of crazy things I did. After I left to go home that evening, I didn't realize they helped me more than I could ever help them. It took a couple of days for me to figure this one out. I had never sat in a chair by a stage watching a rehearsal as Bill Neel. I was watching these ladies perform to see if I had any ideas to improve the show. It could really never be improved if all of their performances were like the one I was watching. They did not have their costumes or make up. It was just everyday folks. They had a (clown) so to speak, in the middle of the stage. A (clown) so to speak, would come from behind the curtain; and when the (clown) behind the curtain was facing the other clown, she would start crying and walk away. Right away, another clown came from behind the curtain and did the same thing. And then a couple more did this. I did not know what was going on. Like "keep listening, Bill." In just a minute or two, they asked why the clowns were crying, and they said – they didn't have anything for the audience. I didn't say much, but I was thinking it needed a little more salt (so to speak). It would keep an audience thinking, alright. It kept me thinking; and I am fair in that department. At first, before I found out what was going on, I thought "I've got part of this figured out." If the clown does not have a name, they can call the clown 'Stinky'. Ha Ha. I went home and started putting all this together. It took a couple of days. I went back to my high-school days. I'd say it was 1954-1955. I was in History class. This was in Altus, Oklahoma (teacher, Mr. Hicks). Mr. Hicks was my favorite teacher. He has passed away. Another man, Ben Hicks (no kin to the first), I knew in England, Arkansas. He put my scrap metals company in the England Democrat paper. He has also since passed away.

Mr. Hicks told us to buy a composition notebook to keep our notes. Now all the other regular books the state furnished. Ok, I bought this book and it belongs to me. It's like if I own a car. I'll paint it any color I want to. Mr. Hicks helped me with my ring a little, too. One day he was in front of the class and he told us not to draw on our notebooks. "Gosh, the guy is a mind-reader," I thought. I had been working on the cover of my book for several days. I wanted to be an artist, but I found out I couldn't 'draw flies'. One day he started walking through the classroom. He came to my desk, picked up my notebook, and he showed it to the class. (Between 20-30 pupils). He said, "Bill, what has this book ever done to you?" (My brain stayed in road gear back then. I'm old now). I said, "I've never done anything to onions, but they make me cry." I knew Mr. Hicks from Middle School also. Years later I had a service station near his home and he was my best ice-cream customer.

Can you see how everything is coming together? As you can see, I knew Mr. Hicks in Altus – a great teacher, and also Ben Hicks in England, Ark. Who helped me a lot. What a coincidence here! After this happened, I found I was not suited for two professions. They would be an artist and a ball player. I can't draw or catch flies. I decided to go with the clown. I was always class clown anyway. Why not get paid for it? All the kids in my class got a big laugh. Keep reading. I will tell you more about the onion ring. It took me just a short time to get this onion ring going. I had remembered buying onion rings at this fast-food place and I liked them. I couldn't eat this one. I tried several different ways to get it to stay on my finger without spinning. Then, an idea hit me; and it worked. I wore the ring doing

Willy the Clown. I was the only clown in the world with an "Onion Ring." It looked like it needed something (no, not salt). *BN*

It just didn't have any "Class." One day I was listening to the radio (the old and reckless). They were advertising this jewelry store talking about diamonds and how many "carrots"! I'm not extra smart. I just listen good. So, what if I can't spell good? I went to East Point. I thought, "Bill, that will help the poor little onion ring come out of its smell." I attached the carrot to the onion, and WHAM!!! I had a One Carrot Onion Ring.

The onion was happy and Uncle Bill was happy.

Bill Neel

Read on for more adventures of:

Willy the Clown and the One Carrot Onion Ring!

Below is a picture of the
"One Carrot Onion Ring"

Above is a picture of the
"One Carrot Onion Ring"

Chapter Seven

"Willy the Clown and the Shirley, Ark. Homecoming Parade"

I'll try not to drag this one out too bad. I'm sure you will enjoy reading it. Reading all of my exciting things I have done keeps me from getting depressed. Everything I write, really did happen. I hope reading all of my material, no matter what subject I wrote about helps you as much as it has helped me. I am not in the medical field; and as you read about the Onion Ring, I'm not in "Right Field" either. Right now, 2016, I am 78 years old. I have a memory better than an elephant. I can remember from my first grade school class until this very moment. I will run out of paper and pens before I run out of funny things for you to read.

Now back to Shirley, Ark. and their Homecoming Parade. I don't perform any longer. I stopped in 2003. I guess I could get a job with the <u>Old and Reckless Radio Show</u>. I didn't have my support dog, Rocky at this time. He is wanting me to tell you folks, he is as smart as two Border Collies. I told him it would be more like three; and he said, "no, just two." He didn't want to brag! With Rocky and I bragging, I'll bet you've already left the parade – maybe Shirley, too. She will find her way home.

Here goes – We all met on the school parking lot. I saw more people there than I had ever seen in Pee Dee. Willy the Clown was minding everyone's business but his own, like usual. Willy looks over and there is the Grand Marshall of the Parade – none other than Ned Perme (weatherman for channel 7 in Little Rock, Ar). Now, guess who had a channel 4 umbrella right close by him – and not a cloud in sight? Willy the Clown told Ned Perme, "Willy had bats in his Bell Free; and he was afraid he would get a tan on that pretty white face; and look like an over-cooked marsh-meller." You know, if you went to East Point, West Point, North Point or South Point, they wouldn't teach you how to "sifer" all that talk that's going on. Ned Perme is a great weather man. You know how you can tell? It's been several years since all this happened, and to this day he is still doing the weather on channel 7 in Little Rock, Ark. Anyone else would have been under the weather (so to speak).

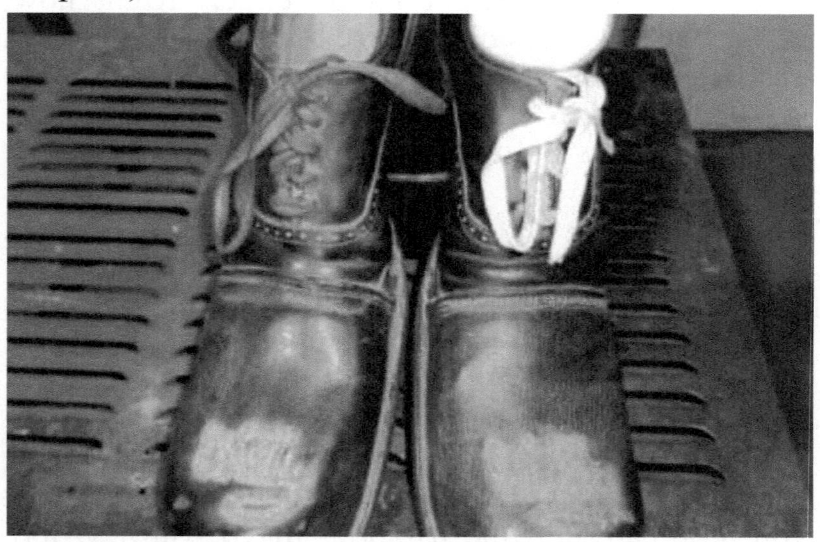

"There was never a dull moment when Willy was around." BN

As we go toward downtown Shirley, there was a little incline; as I start down the incline, I start handing, yes handing kids candy. I never throw candy in the streets with all the stuff up front. I walk over to this young man and his mother. I gave him some candy. He asked me to move just a little. I moved. I thought I was blocking his view of the parade. He asked me to move again. I moved. At this time, his mother and I were wondering what was going on. I asked the young man if anything was wrong. By golly, some of those kids on TV couldn't have beat this. He said, “Mr. Clown, <u>your onion ring is making my eyes water!</u>” I told him I was working on an idea for the carrot in the ring to stop that sort of stuff and let the carrot's eyes water. Maybe I should put a potato on top of the ring. It has eyes. I guess the kids are noticing my “One Carrot Onion Ring” after all.

I made it down close to the Car Wash., and still had my ring. A few minutes later, there were people gathering. They asked me if I had ever been to “Clown School.” I said – “Never been to school in my life.” I didn't say which one.

Willy the Clown

9-1-2016

I'm gittin good at this!

Chapter Eight
"Willy's Fish Tail"
And
"The Adventures of No Not Toe Basco"

During the Shirley, Ar. Festival (South Point), they said they would give $25.00 for the best joke. (Not a joke on the $25.00). I'd have to be Uncle Bill for this part. Uncle Bill can tell funnier jokes than Willy the Clown. I wouldn't keep the money I won. I'd have to get a new boat paddle. As you all remember, this is a joke. When I started telling it, don't jump out any windows or anything. I hope you enjoy this one "2." I have told this joke many times, and for a while I have people believing me. "I made this up." I will always tell you when it's a joke. Anything else really happens in real life.

I won't mention the train bridge. That is where it started, and ended at the highway bridge. Who knows? This might even go to 'Your-Up.' So only the Train Bridge will be changed to protect the guilty. I took my little 12 foot aluminum boat to the big bridge in Shirley, Ark.; put it in the river and hollered "Cast off mate!" Sounds like I never left England. I started my trip to this other old bridge which was about a mile, give or take. Well, I guess you could say "as the fish swims." Now, all I've got is a small trolling motor. It gets me where I'm going, and I get good gas mileage since it works on the 12 volt Bat Tree. (Look this up in my dictionary if you have trouble with this werd or any other you might wonder about. I put this long chain and a perch hook on the end for my anker. I put this perch hook on it just in case they didn't bite my Whale Hook that day. Some days I have caught some so big they would pull my boat back to where my boat trailer is parked and I didn't have to use my trolling motor going back. This day was different. I didn't get a bite fur airs. I decided to go to another spot.

By Golly, I liked to have not got that 50 pound anker up out of the water. I was almost ready to leave the anker there. Then I thought, 'you can't do that; you've caught bigger fish than 50 pounds.' I kept pulling and I got the chain and everything in the boat. I was so gived out. I decided I would get me a fish dinner at one of them 'Fast Marts.' I started back to my boat trailer and I look around, and a big fin was behind my boat. It was all my trolling motor could do, and me trying to paddle. Maybe 2 miles an air. I was so scared.

Are you scared by now?? I got my paddle and beat that fin nearly to death. I started my trolling motor again. I'm too tired to paddle. I was going a mile and a half an air. That was even worse. I lost that extra half mile an air. That fin was still after me. I knew it must have been a big fish since the water in the river was unable to cover it. I finally got to my boat trailer. Oh yes, I gave that monster a few more Licks with my paddle. After taking closer look at the monster, it was my bait. I had forgot to reel my rod and reel in when I started my journey. I was dragging my bait all this way. Usually I try not to get excited. I was so tuckered out from getting that anker in, I forgot my fishing pole. *Bill Neel* 9-1-2016

P.S. What kind of fish did Bill plan to catch??? Have you ever noticed that people who have a boat will fish right next to the bank, and people on the bank want to fish in the middle of the river?

I hope you like my stories. I hardly ever get stressed out anymore. I enjoy sitting at my kitchen table doing this. Looks like I need to stop and work on dirty dishes in the sink.

Bill Neel 9/1/2016

"The Adventures of No Not Toe Basco"

(The Tobacco Kid and his pal Nick O' Teen)

This is an adult western. I hope you like it. I think it's funny. This could be a real situation (er not).

Bill Neel 9-4-2016

It started out in a little town called N-Hail. Don't start laughing and going to find Shirley. I told you she would find her way home. This little town started out with a different name. Oh yes, the State Bird is the Vulture. Back in 1803 this town was full of gunslingers. There were all kinds of seven guns and Rye-fulls all over the streets and saloons. You mite wonder why I put seven guns. If you just rode into town and had a shootout with a local; he would fire at you six times and you would step out in the open to tell him he was out of bullets, and he would plug you like a watermelon. Only the local people knew about the Lucky Seven Pistol Company at the end of the street. Not very many people would visit N-Hail; probably because there were so many guns and rifles laying everywhere. You could hardly walk. Like the locals were the only Gunslingers. Sometimes they would hit the wrong person. Then more Gunslinging would erupt. Almost everyone in town had a lot of Corns on their feet. It was easier to walk that way.

Everybody got along pretty good, I'd say. No killings much. There was one old prospector in town who was always going out to the Hills to look for gold, silver – maybe fools gold and silver. The Hills lived just outside of town. His name was Winston Puffer. He was about as old as the Hills, so age was no barrier. He would walk and pull his mule – Smoky. He would go out there quite often. It was terrible about the noise that mule would make walking on those guns. Now Winston couldn't put corns on Smoky's feet. Corn was reel scarce in N-Hail because it was a popular item.
A lot of the noise was from pots, pans and Dirty Dishes that was on Smoky's back. Sometimes if the wind was just right, you could hear Smoky hollering.

I told you this is an Adult-Kiddie Western. For a long time these couple of gunslingers had their eye on Winston Puffer. He would always carry a little pouch with him and try to hide it when he could. The only Law they had in N-Hail was Out Law. Winston knew he was in deep trouble, and he could only think of two people who could save him. The only weapon he had to fight with was an old beat up Pocket Knife that was about ready to fall apart. That was the worst thing a man could have in N-Hail. As you remember, you had to be a Gunslinger. Pocket knives were only to be used for whit-ling and not slinging. He had set on the board walk in front of the Saloon whit-ling so long some of the Gunslingers would stop slinging and pull Winston out from all the shavings he had made that day. No wonder his pocket knife was in such bad shape. He took all his shavings he had piled up forever and set them on fire. He was sending a Smoke Signal to his friends, the Tobacco Kid and Nick O'Teen. At first the Indians saw the signal and noticed it was a wrong smoker. It was a Long Distance Smoker. Right away the Tobacco Kid and Nick O'Teen saw it was for them. Hardly Two Puffs had went up and the Tobacco Kid and Nick O'Teen were almost half way there.

They lived in a Cave somewhere or another. You could tell I had that right. They looked a little Batty. Winston didn't know his friends would get there so quick, so he got Smoky and started for the Hills, chewing his Bubble Gum and trying to hide his pouch of treasures in his vest! As he got outside town, a couple of Gunslingers were waiting in Ambush for him. They told Winston to give them his pouch. They saw him put it in his vest. They told him it was either the pouch or all of that bubble gum he had stacked all over the pots and pans on Old Smoky. Winston thought it over. It would be just a little bit before the Tobacco Kid and Nick O'Teen would show up. He didn't want to get hit with a Seven Gun. They hurt worse than a Six Gun. He gave them the pouch.

Just as they got down the road a little bit, here comes Winston's friends, and he tells them about the GunSlingers who took his pouch. Right away, the Tobacco Kid and Nick O'Teen had captured the pouch robbers. Winston was so happy to get it back. He almost had enough in the pouch to get what he wanted. If they had gotten away, he could have gone through his pots and pans and the Hills would have chewed him out. After they all got back to town and the bad guys locked up, The Tobacco Kid and Nick O'Teen asked Winston "what was so valuable in that pouch you had with you all the time?" Have you readers been able to guess what was in the Pouch?? It was almost 50 bubble gum wrappers. On the wrapper, it says “Save 50 Bubble Gum wrappers and get a new Barr-Lowe Pocket Knife. Winston had it figured, he would have enough to get it after he chewed all that bubble gum he had scattered in all the pots, pans, and Dirty Dishes on Old Smoky.

Oh, by the way – the Tobacco Kid and Nick O'Teen retired from the Sherriff's Office and now are staying in their cave raising mushrooms. Maybe raising cane too.

Bill Neel 9-4-2016

I forgot to mention. Along with the Gunslinging, there was a lot of MudSlinging too. If you got hit in the arm with the guns and mud, then you would need an arm sling.

Like – “Just a Slinging”

Bill Neel

Rocky is Mad Lee in love with Puff. He has never liked her at all. He doesn’t want to be in the same house with her. The other morning, I woke up and she was cuddled up in bed with him. They are together like this every day. He even lets her sleep on his ‘Green Blanket”. ??? They are sleeping together as I type this. Is it the water?

Uncle Bill, Rocky, & Puff Neel

Chapter Nine

"Mower and Mower"

{Most of this is true!}

I live out here in the middle of nowhere; and I think mower goes on out here than in New York City. I've always tried to keep my yard work around my house looking good. I was in on that little deal in either 1962 or 1963 (Cuba). Hey, I can remember a lot; but not everything. We were all pretty scared about that. All of us that were in on that got out ok – both sides. I have got a project going on at my place right as I write that is just about to get to me. It reminds me of the story about ~~Jack~~ "Bill and the Bean Stalk." (Ha Ha). I have had surgery a time or two in the last year or so. I turned 78 at the end of June 2016. This is now about the middle of September 2016. I've seen and herd a lot during my time. I lived in Pine Bluff and England, Arkansas. That was Rice Country, and also Skeeter Country. I spell it that way because I can't spell (moe-ski-toes). Now, I'm not blaming it all on the Skeeters down here. We don't have any Rice or Water Crest farmers. So, where do I go to now? Well, you might remember ~~Jack~~ Bill's mother sent him to town with a cow to trade her for food and other things. ~~Jack~~ Bill had only been gone just a few minutes, and his mother put her thinking cap on. It looked like one of those night caps?? She thought, "Why, oh why did I let Bill (she was the only one who knew my real name) take that cow to town when we could have opened an Uncle Bill's Steak House." She thought, 'he will probably come back with a two pound bag of Pinto Beans'. She said, "I'll soak him if he does." I had several businesses before, but I did not invest in Beef. I was too tard at the time. I felt like my atomic clock had just exploded. Now back to ~~Jack's~~ Bill's adventure. While I was trying to make some deals with the cow, I met this guy going to St. Ives. I knew he didn't know how to read, cause he had already passed the sign going to St Ives and he was going to Altus, (Not the Wine Country). I stopped him to see if he had anything to trade for the cow. He said, "All I can offer is these Pinto Beans, about 2 pounds; and since he had them soaking for a day or two, it looked like he had 100 pounds of beans. (Over here close to St. Ives, there weren't very many Skeeters. I'll get to the Skeeters in a little bit). I was tard of making deals, so I took him up on his offer. Before he could get out of sight, I herd him screaming. The cow had eaten four pounds of his Pinto Beans he was saving for all them folks he had in his group. Now I came out pretty good. I was already ahead by two pounds. I'm not too good with pounds and ounces of British Money. Why two pounds on that mite be only fifty cents.

I knew my mother was going to tell me I had got a real soaking. I tried to get to the house at night so I could plant these beans by the Moon. I got to plant these soaked beans by the moon alright. A lot of people were there to Moon Me since it was real cloudy. I even ordered a tank car of furt-tee-lizer to boost the mow-rall. All my family was sleeping right through all of this. The mooners were not real bright. Bright lights seem to hurt my folk's eyes.

The next morning, mom woke up and saw this "puny" little bean plant. Overnight it had only grown four or five inches. Mom started throwing Dirty Dishes at me, saying "Don't try to make me think I have already ate with all these Dirty Dishes. I'm smarter than that." I told her to let the little plant grow just one mower night. She finally said, "If it's not any better in the morning, it's going to be a cooked goose or duck – maybe a poke salad. Mom went in the house, and in just a few minutes that plant had grown to eight or ten foot tall. I thought that bean plant is doing ok for what it has to do. It has to lift the giant and his pad, the duck that lay the silver egg; plus millions and millions of moe-ski-toes that is eating the juice from the bean stems.

The next morning we got up and the bean plant was up in the clouds with the giant screaming, "Hoe, Hoe, Hoe." Mom said, "Bill, I'm hungry. Will you go up there and see what the giant has to offer?" She said, "by the way, you mite take some of those little red flashing lights to put on the stalk to keep the planes from hitting it." I grabbed a bunch of Christmas lights and away I went. Just as I started up the stalk, I asked mom - "was this about the same thing that happened to Little Red Riding Hood?" She was about to see Red alright. She said, "Bill, when you get about half way up there, ask the giant what he's got for breakfast." I said, "Mom, what if I can't breathe up there?" She said, "Bill, if the giant can, you can." I got up there, and I asked the giant "what's for breakfast, Pappy?" He said, "Duck eggs, beans and taters, Skeeters on rye and bean juice." I asked him how much for the meal? He said "that will be two thousand pounds." I told you folks before; I don't know a lot about them pounds and ounces. That could be a ton of Money. I told the giant "we will go to a fast food place. They don't deal in Tons of Money." The giant says "wait just a minute. I'm having a sail today. I will give you free food for the rest of yore life." I'm thinking, 'if he falls out of that Bean Stalk, I won't even get my first meal. It would be like my last meal. That would be quite a splash for him to fall with all that stuff he has up there and the 2,000 pounds, if I had it to send.' He finally said, "Uncle Bill, you have something down there I really really need. I can't come down after it, and if I fell, I couldn't get back up here with it. It is so crowded up here, I can't hardly walk anyway." I said, "Ok Pappy, what have I got you are so interested in?" He said, "Bill, I want one of yore Blue Tarps."

Now, Like I told you folks, I'm getting' on up in age, and I've seen and herd a lot of things. This ought to make my herd complete. It's always been on my Bucket List.

I said, "Jolly (sometimes I call him giant or Pappy) – why do you want something so unusual." He said, "every day I look down from my bean stalk and all I can see are Blue Tarps. I would like to look at the green grass, rivers and lakes." Jolly said, "Before I've had two things keeping me from looking at the Seen-Ree. That was yore Blue Tarps and the Clouds. I'm up here - so I can handle the Clouds." I hate to see a Big Giant cry. I told him to send down his clothes-line rope with a few clothes-pens, and I would send it right away. Jolly asked how long it would take to get it to him. I thought, 'well, I've already got to him, but I'll tell him about a weak if he pulls on that clothes-line real hard.'

The moral of this adventure is – 'you never can tell what you're going to git into when you start on one of Uncle Bill's Adventures.' *Bill Neel 9-19-2016*

P.S. This all started with my weeks out of control with tiny mus-kee-toes living in the weeds. They're about the size of nats.

(P.S. Again) Jolly said, after gitting that "Blue Tarp up there, he fixed it up like a flag, so he could tell which way the wind was blowing. Before, if the wind got ruff, he would just ride it out, and a few dirty dishes would fall. This way, he could tell which side of the stalk to stand on. He didn't want to be a stalker. Ha Ha. *Bill Neel*

Above are pictures of Uncle Bill's Sue V Neers that would tell some funny stories – just for laffs!

Chapter Ten

"My Mom's Passing in Altus, Oklahoma"

(She passed away Feb. 18, 2009)

The strange journey back. I don't want to lose this strange thing that happened to me on the way home from Altus, Okla. It's 8 or 9 hundred miles or so. All of this is true 100% I'll spell good too.

Bill Neel 9-22-2016

{Mom – Born 9-22-1916: It would have been her 100th birthday}.

Mom, Annie Lee Neel Perry, moved to Arkansas in the late 1990's. She bought some land in Cleburne County. It was five acers. (many many trees). Mom was the last of my family I grew up with. Delbert B. Neel (dad), Bobby K. Neel (brother) have passed away. I tried to visit Mom every chance I had. I called her every day. If she didn't answer the phone, I would call the police to check on her. I was saying, mom did not like all of the trees. She was raised in the Southwest part of Oklahoma. At night you could see a town 35 miles away. I like the trees. As time passed, Mom's health was getting bad. I tried to spend more time with her as I could. Mom's doctor tried to get her to go to a retirement home. Mom would have nothing to do with that idea. (Mom went back to Altus, Ok.) Mom's doctor tried everything. He finally sent a physicist to talk to mom. He was to prove mom was unable to stay in her apartment alone. Mom was always on the go. She was 91. She would call a taxi to go shopping or ride the church bus on Sundays. She knew the books of the New

Testament, Old Testament, and the Hebrew Alphabet. The Physicist told the doctor she knew more than he did. It wasn't too long until her health put her into the retirement home. I moved into Mom's apartment full time. I went to the retirement home every day. I played games and pushed her in her wheel chair. At about 5pm, February 18, 2009, Mom passed away. I didn't know too many people in Altus, Okla. I had about two weeks to move mom's belongings from the apartment before another month's rent was due. I went to U-Haul and got the biggest enclosed trailer I could find. The man at the U-Haul started not to deal with me when I told him (after he asked) what model pickup I had. I told him it was a 1995 (Ford 150 – 6 cylinder). At that time it was 14 years old. I've still got the little pickup today, September 22, 2016. Now it's 22 years old. I try to take care of my things. So much for that. Oh yes, it's got almost 300,000 miles. I could not find anyone who I could pay to help me. Well, years ago I worked for Ken-Mac Van Lines in Altus, Okla. I can handle most anything. I'm also an Army Vet., and the Lord was helping me too, as you will see at the end of this. I was not feeling very well since Mom had passed away. I was 71 at this time. I might give out, but I never give up. I don't try to rush. I had plenty of time to get this done. I took a lot of breaks. Mom had a favorite chair. It was a Lazy Boy Recliner. I waited to load it last. You remember, I took a lot of breaks. To this day, 2016, I still have Mom's chair in the barn. I had a little problem. I had a few things I could not get in the trailer; so I put these in the bed of my pickup and strapped everything down real, real good. Mom's recliner was one of the items in the back of the pickup. As we go along, you will see how I knew the Lord was with me. I like to drive at night and run with the big rigs. I left Altus and drove to Lawton, Oka – then caught H.E. Baily Turnpike to Oklahoma City. I checked my load just before I got on I-40 to Fort Smith. Everything was really good shape as I drove awhile on I-40, I wondered if Mom's chair was still with me. I stopped a few times to get coffee and be sure everything was ok. Big rigs push a lot of wind. Hey, I'm 71 and acting like I'm 20. I was pretty beat when I got to Fort Smith. I checked the load at Fort Smith and it was still in good shape. I thought, "I'm not going to check the load again until I get to Clinton, Ar. I made it to Morrilton, Ark. And took Hwy. 9 to Clinton, Ark. The sun had been shining for a while. I took Hwy. 65 to Clinton. I needed some gas. I was very very beat now. You remember what I said - "I might give out, but I never give up. Just as I pulled into the station, Mom's recliner came flying out of the pickup and hit the ditch. It was not on the highway; and looked in good shape. I thought, "It's not in the way. I'll get gas, take a break, then I'll worry about that project when I get there. I was so happy. I was almost home. I took a big break and I backed the pickup near the chair. This young man said, "I'll get that in the truck for you." I did not know this person; never had seen him before. I tried to pay him, and he said no, and was glad to help me. I was so tired I didn't know how I was going to get Mom's chair in the pickup. I started on my way, and I turned to go to Shirley, Ark. I look, and the young man is behind me. I thought he must live in the Shirley, Ark. Area. I turned toward Fairfield Bay, Ark., and he turns too. I go past Fairfield Bay and he is still behind me. I went a few more miles and turned on my road. "He turned too," I thought. "He must be a neighbor." I'm getting curious now. I stopped my pickup and he stopped. I walked up to him and he said, "We are going to help you unload your things. I've got my son on the way to help us." Remember how I had to put the recliner in the back of the pickup and it rode almost 1,000 miles (give or take), and didn't cause trouble until I got to Clinton, Arkansas. I'm sure Mom was looking down too. The Lord and Mom knew how tired I was. They helped me a lot. I tried to pay them. I asked them their names. They would not give their names. It's been a few years since this happened. With this being September 22, 2016 and Mom's One hundredth birthday, I wanted to write this today.

I will never forget what you guys did for me. I always try to help people when I can. I know the Lord blesses your families every day. Again, I was 71 then, and I'm 78 now, and I'm still going strong. The V.A. in Little Rock and Conway have also helped me a lot. Also a lot of my friends have been there for me. I try to greet everyone with a smile and ask "how are you?" My little dog, Rocky Neel will not bite you. He minds his master. Thanks again! I'm so glad to be a Razorback.

Go Hogs!!!

Bill Neel and Rocky

Chapter Eleven
"Cars that Go Buy"

I sit here at the house. I haven't seen a car go by in weeks. My family here consists of Myself, Rocky (dog), and Puff (cat). My nearest (people) family live 1,000 miles away (give or take). When I get tired of watching Green Acres or (the Old and Wreckless – Ha Ha), I have live entertainment in my home. Rocky doesn't want me to pet Puff and Puff doesn't want me to pet Rocky. At times I forget to put down on my paper a car passed by. Oh well, I'm still on the first sheet of paper I started with 20 years ago.

I got to go to VA in Little Rock, Ark. In the next couple of days. We see more cars up there in 5 minutes than we have seen here at the home in 20 years. A few months ago there was a rumor that Bill Neel was getting married. You know something funny – after all these years, I have lived on this mountain, nobody knew I have been married (now divorced) and have a daughter in the Netherlands and a son in Cincinnati, Ohio and two sons in San Antonio, Texas. I am a great grandfather.

I used to sell honey at Fairfield Bay, Ark. That was a hobby to separate Rocky and Puff mostly. Puff got a metal folding chair at the flea market – (Ha-Ha) How did Puff get her name? In 1944 when I was in first grade, we had a reader. There was this family – Father, Mother, Dick, Jane, Baby Sally, Spot, Puff, Grandmother and Grandfather. Even to this day I remember most of the kids in my first grade and also all of the teachers I have had along the way. No wonder I started Willy the Clown. I will put this in the adventures I have had. I know I put in the other part of my book about Willy; but in this, I will show you I'm not fibbing when I say I did Wal-Mart opening when they only had a handful of stores. I started with the opening of the Van Buren, Ark. Store. I did this for awhile, and the last store I did was Junction City, Kansas. I could see I was about to lose my family. I did almost all of the new store openings in between these two I just mentioned. To start, there was a Winn Dixie store next to the new Wal-Mart in Van Buren, Ark. Wal-Mart's were closed on Sunday. I'm writing this in no particular order.

As I put before, I was born in Oklahoma. I stayed there almost 30 years. (Like 'Bill, are you a nut case or what??). I got a card to go to Broken Arrow, Okla. I knew where Broken Arrow was – (near Tulsa). I did not fly. I had enough when I was in the service! I was still living in Pine Bluff. As I was going – yes, I was going to Broken Bow. I knew the Indian had broken something or another. Now, my Grandmother was full blood Indian. (This is OK). Now, you can see how my brain works. Some people say they are 6 months ahead of their people. I guess in a way I'm a year and a half ahead of mine. My wife at that time was a seamstress. She made my clown suits. She spoke 5 languages (true). I guess that is the reason we didn't make it. I had a hard time with English (HA HA). I'm thinking, why doesn't Mr. Walton put a Wal-Mart in Pine Bluff, Ark.? I wouldn't have to drive so far. No wonder my mother took me to the doctor to see what was wrong with my brain. I left Pine Bluff real early so I would not be too late getting to (Broken??). When I got there, I usually got a motel room since I'm going to be here a few days. I decided to get gasoline first. I asked the service station manager if he could tell me how to find the local Wal-Mart?? He said, "Mister, the nearest Wal-Mart is Idabel, Okla." Then my real brain kicked in. I thought, 'No!! - Now I was going to have to drive back across Oklahoma.' I called Wal-Mart in Broken Arrow and told them about all of this. They got a big laugh out of that. I thought, "Willy the clown must really be a good entertainer. He is making them laugh before they see him." It took a while to get there. I told the manager I would put on a show for a few minutes even if I was a little late. I was going to be there a couple of days anyway.

When I got dressed and came out, they addressed the audience. "The reason Willy the Clown is late is because he forgot what the Indians broke. Their bows or their arrows." That was cool. Wal-Mart had some good entertainers too. Mr. Walton had this deal he called "a Dry Run." This would be on Monday before the Grand Opening. On Tuesday, not many people in the country had seen anything like this. You could buy things on Monday (the Dry Run). You could go home and tell your friends about what was about to happen on "PRICES." I can't get over it. Some towns were so small, the "skeeters" wouldn't bother to stop. On the Grand Openings, I've never seen so many cars and people in my life. I wrote about people in the country being overlooked. Mr. Walton did not choose his customers. He gave everyone a chance to shop. He did finally have Wal-Marts in the big cities. I did not do the Wal-Mart in Pine Bluff or Altus, Okla. It takes a single person to do what I was doing back in the 1990's. I had moved already to Edgemont, Ark. To retire.

I met these people in my area that did a High-wire Act for Ringling Bros. Barnum and Bailey Circus. I don't want to say their names or location. They are about my age. No, I'm not joking. I'll tell you when I'm joking. Not everyone can do this sort of work (if you call it that. It's more fun than work).

I'm glad I can look back on all of this and recall it just like it was happening today. Every time I get all stressed out from going out to see the rest of the world, I come back and write what I remember, and brother and sister, that is a lot, being 78. The ink is stronger than the stress. Anyone can do what I have done. It's not all about education. I don't mean not to go to college if you can. It has a lot to do with "personality." People can spot that in a minute. Whether you are in business or working for someone, let the people know you are happy. I know that's hard sometimes. You might try something like I do – writing, fishing, sports, or just anything that makes you comfortable for a short time every day.

I don't know how I got off on that. Back to Mr. Walton and Mrs. Walton. I didn't know who she was the first opening. They had the service desk in front, like a crow's nest. The manager and assistant manager would be at the top of the service desk where they had a bird's eye view. Mr. Walton would be on the service desk with a box of chocolate cherries, telling the crowd whoever came the farthest to shop would get a box of chocolate cherries. I would be in the crowd jumping up and down with my big clown shoes. I'm glad that was way back there. I'd be in real trouble today. A lot of the customers would say where they were from. Mr. Walton would ask me where I was from and I would say, "Pine Bluff, Ark." I was always the winner, but never got my chocolates. I noticed every Grand Opening there was a lady sitting in a metal folding chair doing her

"Crow Shaying." I told you, I can't spell. (I can write, but I can't cast a spell) *BN.* She always looked so relaxed and never seemed to let anything bother her. Even my crazy going on and loud clown shoes. I was right there with all of hundreds and hundreds of other people. When they did the Joplin, Missouri Opening, Mr. Walton was late. I did everything except the chocolate cherries. After a while, I went to the break room for coffee. That was the first time Mr. Walton had ever been late for an opening. A few minutes went by and Mr. Walton's pilot came in the breakroom white as a sheet. He said, they had been flying around Joplin, Mo. for a while trying to burn as much fuel as they could. The landing gear would not come down, and it looked like it was going to be a "Belly Landing." It was a small plane with a prop. The landing gear finally came down. The pilot said Mr. Walton was in no problem with all this. I did not copy any of this from Mr. Walton's book. I was listening to the pilot. He was pretty shook up. Later that day, I saw Mr. Bud Walton pushing shopping carts. I did not do openings for a real long period of time. After I put *Willy the Clown* away, I went in business for myself. I retired completely in 1995. I was real blessed to be able to do all of the things I have done, and all of the people I have met.

I forgot one other opening that was real cute – in Springdale, Ark. If I remember correctly, the Wal-Mart in Springdale was on a hill of some sort like a small shopping center. They built a new concrete block building for the New Wal-Mart. They were having a rodeo parade and it couldn't have been planned any better. Wal-Mart was selling these real small motorscooters. It's hard to ride those things with regular shoes. I got to the announcer or whatever you want to call it, and he said "Here comes the Wall-Mart Clown." I was having a lot of fun. In a way, I guess you could say, *Willy the Clown* was Wal-Mart's first greeter.' I would greet the customers and kids coming in and going out. By golly, looks like I started a new set of words.

The Rogers, Ark. Store was in a little shopping center. If you were going too fast, it could have been a drive in. I haven't been there in several years. The last I saw, it was moved across the street to a new concrete block building. There are not too many towns in Arkansas and Missouri I haven't had *Willy the Clown* doing his thing. As I went on with this, *Willy the Clown* was a snake charmer, palm reader, and much much more. One other thing, at the opening and thereafter, they had a lot of different items outside the store. I remember this Lamp Company (can't think of the name). I'll bet you thought *Willy the Clown* was perfect, didn't you? (ha ha). They had a big assortment of lamps inside and outside. I think they were from around the Truman, Ark. Area.

I write a lot. Why? All the family I have in Arkansas are my dog Rocky (Support Dog) and Puff, from the Fairfield Bay, Ark. Animal Shelter. We know most of the officers and Police Chief in Fairfield Bay, Ark. No, we are not bad. They and many more people in the area will stand by you no matter how good or how bad things are for you. (I'll slip this in). It's a little funny I did on an advertising slogan I put together. These words come to me almost every day if I need them. I don't think he used my idea, but it keeps me out of a lot of trouble. Here goes; Joe (not real name) will never hold you up on prices. The only way he will hold you up is if you have a bad leg! (I wrote several more different slogans for him. I didn't hold him up. It was free).

Here I go asking and no matter how old I get, and to this very day, I will keep asking. Why, oh why did they change the logo on the State from "Land of Opportunity?" It was like that when I crossed the State line for the first time I came to Arkansas in 1968. If I had stayed in Altus, Okla., I would have opened Plumbing Shops. My Dad was a plumber. He had his license; but he liked his office in City Hall much better. Now, I'll get back to my favorite topic – Land of Opportunity. There are many hundreds of people in the State of Arkansas who have proved this to be true. Some are Gone while others are there to keep their memories alive. It's like – my parents named me Billy R. Neel. I go by Bill Neel. I've had a lot of people tell me it goes good together. I named my support Dog Rocky B. Neel. He goes to the VA in Little Rock with me when I have to go for check-ups or other. He goes into a lot of other businesses; but he has a big fan club in the VA. Strangers will stop us and say – "What a pretty dog." I feed and take care of him with the very best. He is with me 24/7. Now let's don't forget Puff. You can look at her and see she does not want for anything – except for Rocky to get out of the way when I try to pet her. Can you see by reading all this what I'm leading up to? No matter if I change my name to Joe or whatever – No matter if I change Rocky's name to Pepper or whatever – No matter if I change Puff's name to Baby Sally or whatever – Oh, I almost forgot; Willy the Clown to Clipper the Clown (See how much better I can write Willy the Clown?) I have given out hundreds of my business cards with my picture on the front and my autograph on the back. Last price I had on Willy's Market, they were worth 35 cents. Pretty good, since they started out for free. (ha ha). No matter what you name anything, yes anything, leave it like it is – "Land of Opportunity!!" That way people will know it's the (Reel) thing, like a soft drink I know.

It's bad outside. I'm going to quit while I can see before the lights go out. I like to write. I never get stressed out doing this. You can speak to Rocky and I. We are there to show you not everyone is stressed out and having a bad day. I was like that before I got Rocky. I am real blessed to have him for several years. Not all dogs can handle his job; like not everyone can fly a plane. It takes a lot of training you can check Rocky's record on how he performs in any of the places I have been with him. Oh, if you happen to notice, Rocky has the same color leash as his colors. (Black and white). For a long time I did not let people pet him. Almost everyone asked that question. He is getting older and I am giving him a little more things he can do. If he doesn't overdo it. You can tell when you see him, he is not the average everyday Boston Terrier. You can also tell Rocky and I are very much bonded and have been from the very first day. If you and your dog are not bonded, it's ok. But he or she can't do the work Rocky does. I know it's real hard for him at times. Rocky will never, never, never mess on any floors anywhere or any time. I will say, this is the way he really is – No matter where-ever he may be. He will tell me when he has to go. There has been times he had held it longer than anyone would think possible. You too can be with Rocky's Fan Club. The other day we were in the V.A. Hospital in Little Rock. It was almost time for the doctor to escort me to his area. Rocky had been there for a while. All of a sudden, he had to go. I told the lady at the desk I'd be right back. She told me it was ok. Rocky did his thing, and we got back. They called my name. What about that for timing? He rides the elevators and is real nice. He's been on every floor. I could write a short story about how I got Rocky as a puppy. We won't bore you to death all at once. It is very very interesting how Rocky's life started with me. We won't mention all the names and a lot of the details. Who knows, one of these days, I can hand out two cards instead of one. I do not entertain any longer. These cards are old and they still look good. We hope to see you soon. You can never tell where we may be. You can tell it's us for sure. He has the only leash we know of at this time – black and white – and a very Pretty Boston Terrier. We let a few people pet him now and then. Please ask. Thank you. (Also a collar to match).

Bill and Rocky Neel

P.S. If I write about Rocky, I've got a lot more things to tell you about. *Willy the Clown*

Rocky says “Hi!”

Chapter Twelve
"Rocky"
&
"More Uncle Bill's Funnies"

I just can't put my pen down. I talk about Rocky all the time. Rocky is smarter than any animal on TV or any kind of "Dog or Cat Beauty Pageant." He knows so many tricks. Most of the time he doesn't know which one I want him to do; – Well, unless I've got one of those Treats from the Dollar Store. He goes crazy when he gets one of those chicken, rice and cranberry jerky strips. Only if he's good. Which is all the time. Puff watches TV (true) every so often. She picks winners of ball games and all kinds of stuff. So far she has a real good pickin' average; but I'm not worried about the last one. There is never a dull moment around here. Oh well, back to counting cars tomorrow. It's getting dark outside.

A while back a fellow came by and said he herd I was getting married. I hadn't herd about it myself. I guess it's like one of those surprise parties. I told him later I was going all out on my Honey Moon to Pee Dee, Arkansas and spend the nights in my camper on my pickup. After a few days of watching the Weaver Creek go under the bridge, I would run or drive on into Clinton, Ark., pick us up a couple of burgers at the fast food I first get to. Then on to Wal-Mart to get my wife a wedding gift and a one carrot onion ring. I had to choose between one of them oven gloves or whatever you call them or a cheap salt and pepper set. Well, the oven glove (or whatever you call them) was 16 cents cheaper. So you know what she got. She fainted on the Wal-Mart parking lot after she saw all of the nice gifts I got for her. I guess she wasn't used to anything fancy like that. I will have to admit, I don't usually spend that much on gifts. No telling what she will get for me. Probably Divorce Papers!!

Here is one for Recycling. When I had Neel's Recycling in England, Ark., I had a customer who has a son in Fairfield Bay, Arkansas. I had my little farm within five miles of Fairfield Bay, Ark. I hadn't moved into my "estate," and lacked a few things before I could move in. I was coming to my farm on the weekends. Man, it seemed like the weekends went by real fast. It was before they had electricity in this area. (Way Way Back). This man's son was remodeling his home in Fairfield Bay, Ark. He gave his dad several aluminum window frames to sell to Neel's Recycling. Some of them had glass – others didn't. I put six of the windows in my farm house. I gave him the best price I could. I can't remember the customer's name or his son from Fairfield Bay. Now, how cool is that for Recycling? I was in Recycling before Fairfield Bay Recycling. The windows are still in the house. *BN 2016*

Sitting here at my kitchen table watching it rain, I remember when I first arrived in Arkansas (Land of Opportunity). It seemed to rain day after day. I could see how the boat business would be a good business too. I was still in Pine Bluff (1968) when I heard these people talking, saying "sure has been dry this year." I thought, if it were to rain like this for just one day in Southwest Oklahoma, it would be big Head Lines on the front page of the paper. Oh well, I just happen to think about this crazy business I almost started near Keo, Arkansas. It is about five miles north of England, Ark. The building was already there, and everything I needed to start. Even the

Buckshot Mud all around. No, you are wrong this time. Not Mud Pies. Maybe not too bad of an idea. All you would need to add is water. I can just see my mixers after a few ~~minutes~~ seconds. I always held my Stock Holders meetings at the "Git it and Go" Convenient Store in England, Ark. You would want to get there early so you could hold the smaller pigs. If I was in the Chicken Business, it would be "Flock Holders Meeting." You probably would never go to that meeting.

Uncle Bill's Motto

"Like Make Money, Spend Little."

Yes, by golly, I was going to open Uncle Bill's Cat Litter Company. It had a lot of brothers and sisters. One person said it was going to be a trouble spot. Gosh, how long does it take to teach a cat to use Uncle Bill's Cat Litter? No trouble from most cats. Well, I could see a little problem – if they didn't get Uncle Bill's Cat Litter. With the proof of purchase seal, you could bring your cat to the meeting. You might have to look under the lost and found section. One guy at the meeting said he could sew sacks. (This is all for real). There were several people at the meeting ready to go to work. Before I could get this going, my health was not in my favor. I was saying at the very beginning of my life – I had a serious kidney problem. As I got older, it was a small problem every now and then. I didn't get this business going. I had to retire. My kidneys failed me in 1995. I was in V.A. Hospital in Little Rock, Ark. So long I thought I lived there. I spent a lot of time in I.C.U. They thought they were going to lose me. My face looked like a skeleton. It was so bad I didn't recognize myself. They had all of my family by my bed. Well, here it is 2016, and I just might open Uncle Bill's Cat Litter Company after all. No, I'm kidding. Age has caught up with me. All this time since I left V.A. Hospital, I have to get regular checkups. My Renal Doctor told me a couple of months ago, I might live into the three figure digits. I owe everything to the Lord and V.A. I tell people I turned 78 at the end of June 2016. Some say "you are just a youngster." I don't tell them I wasn't to live past ten years old. I am so glad I came to Arkansas, the Land of Opportunity. I feel like I am a real Razorback now!

Go! Hogs! Go!!! *BN*

I will say real quick why I was not to open the Uncle Bill's Cat Litter Company. It rains so much. I could have been stuck in the Buckshot Mud so bad I couldn't get out. After I passed on, they could have made a bronze statue of me (real life-like) in front of Uncle Bill's Cat Litter Company. Popeye wouldn't hold a candle to me. I would have the real me in my statue. People would think I went back to Roswell, New Mexico and took off for another adventure. At least they couldn't kidnap me. If they tried, they would be stuck in the Buckshot too.

I will always call England, Ark. my home town. I wish I hadn't sold the Old Neel Building. I think right now, I would put another business in the old building. I would call it Ann-Teeks. I could handle a job like that. I have a lot of Ann-Teeks I have collected over the years. Oh yes, my mother's name is Ann. She would have been 100 years old Sept. 22, 2016. The reason I put Ann after my mother's name – it's Ann on her marker, and it will always be Ann Neel.

I'm going to tell you a real good funny. This really did happen in Little Rock, Ark. I can't remember what year this happened. It was in the mid to late 1980's. Somewhere in all of my "Ann Teeks," it will finally show up. I got an invitation to attend a Reynold's Aluminum Meeting in Little Rock, Ark. No "Git and Go" in England. I'm not going to be like my Boston Terrier (Rocky) and tell you I went to East Point. Do you get the Point?? There were people from all over the U.S. – even Bill Neel from England. Now over a period of time, I had really worked hard with my British accent. I knew one day my hard work would pay off. You know Chap, I fine-lee got pretty good with it. As I went into the meeting, a young lady from South Carolina was passing out these "Hello, I'm Mr. or Mrs.--" stickers.

Now would you believe my Horror-Scope Book says I'm real quiet and keep to myself? I'm sure you read the part where I threw my Horror Scope Book away and wrote another one. I'll probably have a pile of them books pretty soon.

Now back to our adventure. You don't need to send any cash. When she came to me, the "Hello" sticker took on a new meaning. She asked me where I was from. I told her "England." Before I could say "Arkansas," she was real excited, and said "You're from England!" I was probably in my 40's and I was going to put England on the map. (A real pretty young lady). I started talking to her with my British accent. She said, "How did you ever find us?" I told her I was visiting Little Rock, Arkansas, and I saw all of these cars and people; and I had to check it out. A lot of the people were waiting on their "Hello" stickers; and listening to the "man from England" (or uncle). Nobody was getting upset. Even later when they found the truth, nobody got mad. We all had a good time. Now days, they would have said, "The British are coming" and call the bomb squad. That is one reason I'm doing this. I write and read my adventures on my kitchen table; and I am writing and laughing so much, I don't have time to be depressed. I have mentioned this a time or two. I hope this helps you as much as it has helped me. Like I said before; I'm not in the Medical Field or not in Right Field either. All of a sudden, this man I knew who was with Reynolds Aluminum came by. He said, "Bill, what are you doing?" The lady spoke up and said "this man is from England." My friend told her, "yes. It's England, Arkansas – about 25 miles down the road." Everyone started laughing. I keep telling everyone - "laughter is the best medicine." Keep reading Uncle Bill's stories and you will see, I can never be an Uncle. My only brother, Bobby K. Neel was killed in a car accident in 1961; and I have no sisters. I made myself an Uncle. Years ago I would walk on the sidewalks in England, Ark. window shopping. Most of the younger people would say, "Hi Uncle Bill." Maybe that is the reason I kept hanging in there with my medical and other problems. I thought at this time I didn't have family in Arkansas; but I had more family than anyone in town. If you have never been to England, it's only a few miles from anywhere in the world you might be. If you fly into Little Rock, Ark., and your plane is going to be delayed awhile, you can see England without getting jet lag. Well, maybe car sick. When I lived there, we had -The London House, Queen of England, Bank of England and several townspeople who could speak

British very well. There was a famous Okie who said, 'All he knew was what he read in the newspaper.' (Will Rogers). Uncle Bill said, “All he knew was what he saw on T.V.” Uncle Bill also said, “It might be better to read the England Democrat.”

Bill Neel, Willy the Clown, Rocky Neel,

and

Puff Neel

BN 2016

Rocky is Mad Lee in love with Puff. He has never liked her at all. He doesn’t want to be in the same house with her. The other morning, I woke up and she was cuddled up in bed with him. They are together like this every day. He even lets her sleep on his ‘Green Blanket”. ??? They are sleeping together as I type this. Is it the water?

Willy the Clown

“Orkansaw Anglish:”

Deduce – what you play after de-ace.
Deface – what to cover when throwing pies

Chapter Thirteen
How I Got to Know Rocky, the Wonder Dog
{This is a True Story}
By: Bill Neel 10-25-2016

It was about the middle of 2013. I was walking my three mile trip to highway 16 and back to "Bell-E-Akers." At first it was Fowl-Play-Akers. The hawks took care of that. I started Belly Akin a lot about those birds speeding. Oh well, it gave me another name for my ranch. This name seems to be right. It is now October 2016, and it's still Bell-E-Akers.

Now back to Rocky the wonder dog. My grandson had just left to seek his fortune. Also, his last going away party. It would be ok if he got a job as a Dish Washer. He wouldn't have to look at all the Dirty Dishes. He had to leave his dog, Ace. Ace will also be in my book. It's a real sad story about Ace; and his cat. A lot of people have said it was Ace who invited Rocky to visit him (so to speak). Ace would walk with me every morning. I didn't have him on a leash. We hardly ever saw a car until we arrived at the highway. I would never never let Ace on the highway. Ace would visit everyone along the way. Ace was not a pointer – he was a smeller. Oh, at the words I come up with. That nose was always close to the ground and running. One day Ace and I came home. It was like any other day. About a couple of hours later, I noticed a cute little Boston Terrier in my yard. If this was true about Ace inviting (Jack) Rocky to Bell-E-Akers, I could understand. (Jack)

Rocky's little legs were not able to keep up with us, and it took him a couple of hours to get here. He was really that small. You will notice (Jack) in several places in our story. You will see after a while, this was, I will say again- a real important word. No, it has nothing to do with a beanstalk. We have that in another story. – Mush, you Terriers. Now back to Rocky the Wonder Dog. I had never seen such a pretty little puppy. I didn't want to get attached to him. Yes, it was a “him.” I thought, I had sung my last him when my grandson left. Ace had the three cats. I guess he couldn't speak cat too well and now he has someone to communicate with. I just knew any day someone was going to claim him. I put flyers everywhere. I would show him to people. No one seemed to know anything about him. He didn't have a collar, no tag or anyone claiming him. *(Thought)*
'Oh no – did he come from Roswell too?' (HA HA)
In a short while (Jack) Rocky started walking to the highway with Ace and I. He began to keep up with us pretty good. I would not let (Jack) Rocky on the highway. It's a wonder he listened to me. If you teach man or beast, the teacher has to be smarter than the student. Ace was doing a better job at this. They both spoke the same language. Ace would still run with that nose close to the ground. We would be at the highway for a minute or two, and then go home. As I put in parts of my book, I hardly ever get depressed. I'm so busy laughing, I don't have the time. A short distance from the highway, there was a beautiful home. It had been there for a good while. I saw it built from the ground up. I know for a fact after I found out who lived there, this home would feature my grandson, and (Jack) Rocky before it was all over. I really enjoyed my walk to the highway every

morning. All of a sudden, it was like two years had gone by. I didn't think about where Rocky had come from anymore. I had taken real good care of him. I took him to the vet. Regular. He had a collar and a tag. I get his teeth cleaned. He bonded with me more than any dog I had ever had in my life. Rocky came to me just when I needed him; and the way it looked, Rocky needed me. He had passed three homes on his way to my house. I found out later, he was not happy where he was living and always running away. He was going along the highway and people knew where he belonged and would bring him home. When he came to the bottom of the mountain, I had no clue where he was from. One day, Ace, Rocky and I was about to go home from the highway, and the man who lived in the beautiful home wanted to show us something he had. My friend Steve, who had some property farther down from me was with us, and we all went over to check it out. Even Rocky the Wonder Dog. His home was a short distance from our turn-around spot. As we walked to his home, he said, "Where did you get that Boston Terrier?" I said, "He came to my house two years ago." He said, "That is my dog." I told him, "Well, you can have him back only if you pay two years groceries and vet bills." He looked like he had been hit with a Blivvet (we used that word in the army back in 1961 and years after. Don't ask about the word – just accept it). My grandson, sometime before this - was always having trouble in school. I spent more time at school than my grandson. I would have never guessed where Rocky was from. Not only that, as time went by, I found out what Rocky's name was before I changed it. My horror-scope says I can bide my time until things are better. One day I took Rocky to the vet. There was a man in front of us waiting. He said, "That dog looks familiar." He said, "That's Jack." I don't know how many times I have taken him home. I told him his name is now Rocky. He said, "come here Rocky," and petted him. He said, "You have finally found a good home." That was so touching. It's not over yet. Will this be a good movie? We have a lot more to tell you. None of this is made up. It's all true. It was always exciting to watch Rocky and Ace with their noses to the ground – like four eyes are better than two. One day, as we were walking home, Rocky and Ace were "Big Game Hunting" so to speak. They found out real quick that the little game gets real exciting too. When it was all over, Uncle Bill had to help them with a big stick. The brush was not real high in this large field; and Rocky and Ace thought they were the "Kings of the Field" until, yes, until they spotted two real young (well, it wasn't Mellon Collies – HA HA). I can't find the right word 'Cyote' in the dictionary, so I will call them Mellon Collies Ha Ha, and let it go at that. They were not hungry. They just wanted to play. If this had been their parents, it would look like a fast-food – Hot Dog Place. Well, it all started out as play and games. The cyotes began to get a little serious. Ace began to scream. He and Rocky were running faster than any horse ever in the Kentucky Derby – yes, any horse. I found a large tree limb. Rocky and Ace ran right by me. When the coyotes saw me with the big stick, they decided to go find someone else to play with. Did Rocky and Ace learn a lesson from this ordeal?? Did Uncle Bill learn a lesson? – I guess not. He got back into a bigger mess than that. I always get a few days break before Rocky and Ace could stir up something. Like this was an ordinary day to start with. Little did

I know, this was going to end with "Fowl Play." Never a dull moment. As we were walking to the highway, there was this culvert in the ditch to this house, so the people could drive over it and keep the water flowing in the ditch. Well, it hadn't rained in a good while and someone had a family inside this culvert; and they didn't want to be disturbed. These are real mean critters when you get their feathers (rouled) up. These birds are serious except when it comes to Thanksgiving or Christmas. It's mostly their tame cousins you see on the table. I had never had a fight with a wild turkey before. This is all true. Everything I am writing, (How I got to know Rocky), I am putting it down from the time he came to my house until now – Oct. 2016. I will let you know when I'm joking. These mother birds with their babies will take on man or beast to protect their family. I'm looking eye to eye at a mother turkey. When we were walking by, going to the highway was just a little warning. Rocky and Ace nose was always getting them in trouble. As we were coming back from the highway, Rocky and Ace just had to give the mother turkey some "Good Advice." It would have been better to keep walking.

I don't think she needed any advice. She had plenty of time to think about the advice she had gotten from us a few minutes earlier. We were not on our game plan as good as she was. Just before the culvert, Rocky and Ace had it all planned out, they thought. The mother turkey came rushing out like she was on fire. I guess that is the right word to use. She was pretty hot alright. We are not talking about a 90 pound weakling. Rocky and Ace didn't have time to scream as fast as they were going. They were more scared than they were on the last games they were playing.

They ran behind me, Like "Uncle Bill, get your big stick." I had never been this scared before. I didn't think all of this would get this much out of hand. The turkey ran at me like I was the matador at a bull turkey fight. These birds won't act like this unless they have babies. She hit me on the leg on her first pass. I am getting real scared now. I can't find anything to defend myself. I couldn't take my eyes off this big bird. She was not fighting the right deal who started all this mess. I could just see Rocky and Ace sitting back there in the stands, eating popcorn and cheering me on. I was getting a raw deal. The matadors always have a sword. I didn't even have a pocket knife. She came at me again. I gave her a little kick as she went by – not enough to hurt her. I let her know I was not taking any more. At this time, Rocky and Ace ran by, going home. If the cops had been there, they would have gotten a ticket for speeding. All of this distracted the Mother Turkey and gave me a chance to be on my way. I wasn't running, but I was walking pretty fast. I knew she wouldn't get too far from her babies. You think I'm finished talking about Rocky and Ace, don't you?

Oh no – this one is cute and funny. A few years ago, I saw this movie about a small boy, his dog, and Mom and Dad. Keep these words in mind. These same words will appear again. The young man has to move to another state with his mom and dad on a better job. The young man has a dog named Pete and these two were bonded like Rocky and I. They were not able to take Pete right away; and left him with a friend. It was really upsetting for the boy and the dog. Dad told the boy they would be back to get Pete in a few weeks. The family had moved several hundred miles. The family didn't know, but Pete had escaped from the friend's house soon after his master left. The little boy was always worried about Pete. He thought Pete was with their friend. The friend was scared to call and let the little boy know Pete was gone. A couple of weeks or so went by and Dad told the boy they would get Pete in a few days. One day just before they were going to get Pete, he was coming home from work. He saw a long line of cars stopped on this exit he took every day going home. He thought it was a bad car accident, and got out of his car to see if he could help. As he walked down the road, he could see he was really the only one who could help. Pete had taken the exit too and was blocking cars. Pete had made it somehow to within a couple of miles of where his master lived. Animals are smarter than people at times. The man got Pete and put him in his car and finished Pete's journey home.

Now, you can see what happens if your dog or cat are bonded to you. When Dad came home with Pete, his son could not believe all this. Pete had traveled several hundred miles. I wrote this to show how strange things happen.

I have some friends who live farther down from me. They have a dog and didn't need another one. Someone had dropped off a Pomeranian. Most always you have to buy these dogs. I guess this would soon be Uncle Bill's discount. They called me; and I tried to tell them I was already in the Dog House – so to speak. Crazy me – here I go again. Ace would never ride, and I couldn't open the door to the pickup fast enough for Rocky. I look at this little dog and I can already see the handwriting on the wall. Those little legs would be a major problem for him, as active as Rocky and Ace are. Someone had taken

real good care of him. I would never find out very much about him. Yes, I'm singing another him. I don't mean to talk bad, but his little legs didn't look as long as some of those go-fur matches. I have mentioned these matches from time to time in my book. If you have never seen any of these matches, they are pretty small. No, I did not name him Go-fur. That is a cute name alright. I named him “Pete” - after the dog in the movie. He would walk a short distance from the house. He never made it to the highway. Most of the time, I would carry him. One night a big snow storm came. Are you beginning to get the picture? We didn't let anything stop us from our walk. I was trying to get out of the house and leave him where it was warm. Rocky and Ace were running and playing in the snow, having a good time. As we got started on our walk, Pete was in the house screaming and crying. It was real loud for such a little dog. Like they say - “Dynamite comes in small packages.” I went back to get him. He was so happy and excited. I carried him to a spot to where he could walk a little in the snow – like the big boys. I turned my back for a minute, and turned around to check on him, and he had gotten into a snow bank. All you could see of him was his little nose, and not much of that. I grabbed him and took him to the house. Rocky and Ace were still walking and playing. I hated to do this. It really broke my heart. I had gotten attached to Pete and he had gotten attached to me. I knew this wasn't the right home for him and it wasn't right for me to raise him this way. I bit off more than I could chew. I called the Animal Shelter nearby and told them what I had; and also, I couldn't raise him proper. I would never drop off a dog or cat or any other type animal in the middle of no-where. They put Pete in a small cage and he started crying. I started crying too. I tried not to show it. Again, that was the hardest thing I've ever had to do. I know he was in Good Hands. I would never get to see him again. This has been two or three years ago; and it still touches me. A few weeks went by and I went to the Shelter. I asked them about Pete. They said he didn't stay at the Shelter very long. A man, woman and a little boy took him to a good home. I felt better about this. Remember the movie about Pete? He belonged to – a man, woman, and little boy. It is really something how I have things happen to me.

I just can’t quit bragging about Rocky. Every time we go to the VA he keeps adding more people to his list of followers. As we were going to the pick-up, there was this young couple trying to get a young German Shepard in with them, he was wild and looked like no training. Rocky walked on by like he didn’t see him. That put a feather in Rocky’s cap. Sorry I’m bragging too much, he just seems to get better with all the things he was trained to do as time goes by. *BN*

Ace and Thomascena,

A Short Story You Will Never Forget

By Bill Neel

In 1999 a wild cat came to my home. She would not let me get close to her. I thought it might be good for her to be here to keep the mice away. I live at the bottom of a mountain in the Edgemont, Arkansans area. Maybe one car every two months comes by my house. The reason I put this down will be part of what happened as we continue. After a short while, she had kittens under my house. I could hear them crying every now and then. A few days later the mother cat got killed. I could not see these little kittens die. I got under the house and found three kittens. They were all the same color and later found out, they were all female. I went to the Vet in Greers Ferry and got a small bottle and found what sort of formula I needed to raise them. If she had raised these kittens they would have be wild. As time went by, I had the cats spayed. I didn't need any more pets. I named them Diana, Thomascena, and Glade.

Now this may sound boring to some, but what happens in the next few years is like a movie. After a while, Diana leaves and now it's just Glade and Thomascena. Glade demands a lot of attention and Thomascena is like her mother – "wild." Thomascena has little to do with anyone or anything. My grandson had a small puppy; it was a Chow. He moved away and now I was the owner of a puppy. To tell you truth, I was not real happy about this. I didn't know this at the time but, later on, it would change my life. By now the cats where about four years old and they were not happy with this new family member. I wish I had taken pictures at the start of this relationship. It went on so many years. I really didn't think about it. It was something that happened every morning for several years and at this time I never dreamed this would touch me so much. As I mentioned at the beginning of the story. I live at the bottom of a mountain in the Edgemont area. In 1995, before I had the cats or dog, I would walk from my house – pulling two steep hills to the highway (16) and back. I still walk this today in 2014. It is about a three mile trip. I'm sure a lot of people saw me making my turn at the highway every morning to come back home. After I got my grandson's dog, Ace, after a while he started walking with me. We would leave the house about 6 a.m. and would return from our walk about 7 a.m. You could almost set your watch by it. As time went by, just as Ace would get almost home, Thomascena would be in the road to greet him. She would rub on him and Ace would go on to the house.

She was there to greet him just before 7 a.m. every morning. I could not believe this. She didn't have anything to do with anyone else. One day I noticed that Ace showed Thomascena that he was glad to see her. This went one every day for years. Crazy me, I did not get any pictures of this.

In July of 2013, Thomascena and Glade died on the same day. They were about 14 years old. I guess I had done a pretty good job of taking care of them. Ace saw me put Thomascena in the ground and he tried to dig her up. I had to put cement on the grave. The first day, he laid on the grave for about three hours. Every day after that he would visit for a while. Ace was never the same dog after this. I began to take all kinds of pictures. I took pitchers of him on or near the grave. After a month or so, I got him a kitten at the Fairfield Bay Animal Shelter. At first, it didn't go too well. As time went on, he bonded with the kitten. One day I came in the house and he had the kitten between his front paws sleeping in the recliner. After a period of time, the kitten had nothing more to do with Ace. Ace started to go downhill. He wouldn't eat or drink and just lay on his pallet in the Living room. I finally got him to eat a frankfurter and drink a little water. After a few days, he stopped eating again. Even as weak as he was, he would go on a walk with me. I was all torn up inside. Then on March 5, 2014, I got a phone call and as I was putting the phone away, Ace got up from the pallet and ran out the door like someone was outside. I went out to see what was going on, and just as Ace left the front door, he made a left turn toward the pet cemetery and collapsed, taking his last couple of breaths going in the direction of Thomascena's grave. I put him as close as I could to Thomascena. The ground in this area is teal rocky and it's hard to dig in some spots. It was really something, when I dug the grave, I did not find one rock. Like that is where he was to be. At the end of June 2014, I will be 76, and I'm still going on my walk. I have a Boston Terrier who walks with me, but Ace will always be there on the walk with me too.

It all started with me coming to Arkansas (Land of Opportunity) with an ink pen and a map.

Bill Neel 10-25-16

Oh yes, I forgot to tell you: Rocky and I were shopping at a Department store and a lady asked if she could take a picture of Rocky. Are we good or what????

Rocky 10-18-16

"Orkinsaw Anglish:"

Em-bark – what they ask about your dog.

Bill Neel

What Makes Rocky So Special

I don't know how to start this. It's a true story. I want to tell someone. This is extra hard to do. I don't want these people to think bad of me for writing this. Like I have said many times, when I first came to Arkansas I had to start on the ground floor. I'm going to try not to drag this out. I am a soft hearted person and already a little tear has come in my eye. I hate repeating this. Well look at all the shows on TV. I said at one time a person will complain he has no shoes and later see's someone with no feet. At times I get the wrong road and I see what I have just written and I try to forget my small problems. It's hard not to think about your problems until you see a young man in a wheelchair. A family that has just lost their home to a fire on Christmas day and lost everything they had. All of the family survived. They could have lost family members. I had a man with new shoes to trade his shoes for my old shoes. That's when I first came to Arkansas. Land of Opportunity. I don't see the young man in the wheelchair very often. He has a lot to be thankful for too. It can always be worse.

I want to tell this about what Rocky did. I'm very blessed the Lord sent me this dog. He keeps me on the right track more than anyone will ever know. He can tell real fast when I am having problems. Seems he can tell when other people are having problems too. I walk with Rocky in several different areas. In my area, Shirley by the ball park, Fairfield Bay walkway to Jack's Convenience Store, then behind the Dollar Store in Clinton, Arkansas, and Little Rock in the V.A. area. When I get to one of these places I put a leash on Rocky and let him lead the way. If we are in our area he doesn't need a leash and he can run and have a good time. He never gets out of my sight in case I might have trouble of some sort. A very smart dog. I put several places I walk Rocky so that not one place we walk will stand out where this happened.

Rocky and I start walking. He begins to take me to an area we hadn't visited in several months. Not a real popular place for us. I wondered about this at first. Like, I just go with Rocky. More people know Rocky then Uncle Bill. We sit on this bench, I mean Uncle Bill sits on this bench. I'm taking a little break before we finish our journey.

There was some people there and you know Uncle Bill how bashful he is???? I don't know these people. I start talking to them. They were so friendly. Not often do you see this. As we were talking they were telling me how their home burned to the ground last Christmas Day and they had lost everything. That happened over three months ago. I hadn't heard anything about it. They were not asking for anything and already had built a home. This really touched my heart. I've said this in my first book and many times before. I try to help people all I can. Also I have said many times you don't have to find me, I Will Find You.

I tried to write this as to where I would not upset anyone. *BN*

P.S. After a while Rocky was ready to walk again. He didn't want to go any farther. He took me to the pickup to go home. It's like he had done his good deed for the day.
Again!
You don't have to find me… I Will Find You!

Bill Neel & Rocky

Chapter Fourteen

"Rocky the Wonder Dog with Two Much Time On Our Hands"

The other day, I told Rocky we were going on another outing. I said, "It will be several airs before we can leave on our trip. I told Rocky I had to git my clock on my cheap little phone fixed. No, it's not my bat tree. My bat tree has about as much spark as I do. I guess you could compare it with one of them go-fur matches. You know something. I haven't seen any of those matches in years and years. The reason they called them that was you would strike one and Go-Fur another one. During this time, many, many people quit smoking. All of the people trying to light up were smokin' more than their cigarettes. Now, back to the repair on my phone. It will cost me as much as $1.50 to get it fixed. I could get another phone with the $1.50 and have change left. Rocky said to "keep the phone I have." He said he never seen two cans with a piece of wire in them, and only about two foot apart. Most phones like that would have a sun dial. You know I got to thinking about the time I almost got married and gave my almost Bride all those lavish gifts. I think the phone would have tied the knot. We would always be real close together – even when we talked on the phone. When she fainted on the parking lot, I could have called her an ambulance. She would scream, "Call me an ambulance – Call me an ambulance." I said, "ok, you're an ambulance." She hit me with the oven mit I got for her. I'm sure glad I didn't git the salt and pepper shakers. Rocky is getting mower jealous by the minute listening to this. I think I know why my phone is so messed up. Well, it's not Rocky. I was always callin' this lady, and she would give me the time, temp., and a commercial. I had to call this lady a lot since I couldn't tell what time it was on my sun dial at night. Me quitting in the middle of the first grade didn't help either. The poor little phone was worked to death and the lady was getting tired talking to me, thinking I was flirting with her. Finally I told her I was going to get me a "grandfather clock." I could see the numbers ok during the day and use my Go-Fur Matches at night; and I would stop bothering her every couple of minutes. She said, "why don't you git you a "wrist watch" like everyone else?" Then she gives me a big cussing and says she is quitting her job giving the time and temp. She just couldn't take it any longer. It turned out to be my X Bride. I've still got the oven mit she threw at me. I just love happy endings.

Bill Neel 10-11-2016

Since I have the oven mit, I started (or almost started) my marriage with, will I say I am about to git married again? Who Nose? I just No that Lucky Girl is out there somewhere. I already have my gift for the next Bride.

Bill Neel 10-11-16

Chapter Fifteen

"Toe Main Poyson" & "Small Houses"

{More Uncle Bill's Funnies}

By: Bill Neel

Once or twice a-pone a time, now my granny all-ways called it (a pone of bread); but this is a-pone a time. There was this teenage girl who was (always) trying to make the very best choc-lit chip cookies. As you can see fur yourself, her spellin' wasn't much better than mine. All though, I did try to help her. She had some older sisters that was always makin' "Uncle Bill's Fresh Water Taffy." They finally tried Uncle Bill's ress-a-pea cause theirs had two much salt and it left a bitter taste in the customer's mouth. Her name was Sender-Rella. Her sisters were Snow White Rella, Little Red Rella and Taffy Rella. Back then, they weren't any baby books with all kinds of names you could choose from. By the looks of the names for these girls, that is probably why someone came up with the Baby book. They did have one boy in the family. His name was Pee-Noke-key Rella. You thought I was going to put Owe on that boy's name, didn't you? I would have, but they just made the last payment for him at the hospital and now he is a Rella – weather he likes it er knot. The parents were, Old Man Rella and??? She ran away before I started this adventure, saying she could knot take it no mower. Someone said she was "A-Busised." There goes my spelling again. Take it with a grain of salt, that was taken out of the Taffy. Sender didn't let that bother her from making her cookies. Her dad took some of the cookies and put them in the forrest, and told all of them to go look for Easter cookies.

Now, grandma herd about Sender Rella's cookies. She wanted Little Red Rella to bring her cookies. She said, "all them other girls would eat all the cookies before they got to grandma's house." Now, she didn't want Pee No Key Rella, cause he couldn't tell the truth if his nose depended on it. It was already over 2 foot long. Now Sender and the other girls – all they thought about was them barn dances and buying dancing shoes made out of anything but glass. They all herd that those glass shoes would bring you bad luck if you were wearing them and the King would come to the dance and turn you into a pumpkin with a mouse inside; and tell you to git home the best way you could. Not only that, he told them if they were wearing the glass shoes, he would kiss them with an apple in his mouth. It was such a long kiss, all of the girls he kissed would fall over on the floor. Everyone thought they passed on or own. Little did they know, if they had bought a pair of glass shoes and throwed them at the King and hit him in the right place, he would have been so much out of it, he would have taken all the glass shoes and put on a blindfold and picked out a pair of those glass shoes and took one of the girls and married her and she would live happily ever after. Well, the King was also a Mooner, and not very bright. He always had a little light on the subject. You will never guess how big of mess this turned out to be or not to be. There were a lot of girls at the dance. Can you just see about a hundred glass shoes coming at you? The King could not see who hit him where?

And to add insult to injury, all the glass shoes were the same size. Now this King was not about to set there all night and half the next day trying to see who's foot matched the shoes. To this day, the King is single. He doesn't go to those Barn Dances, and he keeps his shoes under the bed the bears didn't want.

BN 9-27-2016

"Small Houses – Can they get to small?"

This is true. Even though it mite be hard to believe. In the last couple of years, I have seen these homes appear almost everywhere. I guess the next size smaller <u>wood</u> be a <u>Pup Tent</u>. Since I put "<u>Pup Tent</u>," I will also add this to the story I started. There are some people down the way who have a nice size dog house that has heat and air. <u>I'm not joking</u>. <u>I have seen it.</u> It's real cool. I would get Rocky one of these; but I don't want his house to look better than mine. I really don't think Rocky would let Puff stay in the house. As I get to looking at all this, if I did git Rocky the house, it <u>wood</u> be a total disaster. He would want me to buy a better house – thousands of dollars, a new pickup – thousands of dollars, all new furniture– thousands of dollars– mower land for my

New Castle – thousands of dollars. Don't fur-git taxes, which <u>wood</u> also be thousands of dollars. Can you just see what can git started from a Pup Tent. I am always in the Dog House. In a short while Rocky and Puff wood be in the castle. I'm sorry I got off on the wrong road. I'm good at that sort of thing. Now back to the Small Houses. I go a few miles to get gasoline fur my pickup. Now being a 1994, it's on a special diet too. Like I said before, I see this small house on my journey. I don't pay the small house a lot of attention. They may add a few small things to the house from time to time. I didn't go by this house for a week or so. As I was going by this time, I couldn't help but notice they had put a garage for their car next to the small house. If you really wanted to git technical about the whole thing, I think the garage was a little bigger than the house. Again, look what a Pup tent can start.

Bill Neel 10-13-16

Rocky woke up to a big surprise this morning. No Puff didn't have Kittens! Well, Puff has been acting funny the last few days. I got a picture of this too. Rocky sleeps late and does not have time to look at Puffs Surprises. Have you noticed how I can Drag these Mysteries Out? Maybe it's because I have Author-Write-Us. Oh well, Rocky says to go ahead and embarrass him. Next to Rocky's bed was a little dead mouse. Rocky said it might be OK under GLASS. *Uncle Bill, Rocky, & Puff Neel.*

Chapter Sixteen

"Just Some Stunts for the Kids"

{Snake Charmer}

Get a wicker basket with lid. (Try to find a wooden flute). Get all the kids around the basket. They are not to make a sound while you are playing. It gives the snake head-akes if he hears any noise except for Willy playing the flute. Keep playing until you can hardly stand it. Before we go any further – Not just anyone can play a flute and make a snake rise out of a wicker basket. When Willy the Clown first tried this breathtaking stunt, he used all of the yeast this big grocery store had. Even with all that musical talent and the fast rising yeast, the lid hardly moved. As you noticed, at the beginning of all this mess, it looks like one of granny's res-a-peas. So much for that. As time went on, Willy would play his flute fur Airs. It began to drive the white mice and rats away. Oh yes, Willy was not doing the right thing. He was not wearing the right color toe bog-in. We will let you guess what color the snake wanted to see Willy wearing. One day, Willy had made so many excuses for "N-the Grass." Well, I've herd worse names for snakes. He had to help "N-the Grass" not to feel so cooped up. One night Willy opened the lid, and you have never seen such. It was like this lady who would say to this magic pot- "Boil" – and the pot would make her family some real good soup. Then she would say "Pot stop" – and the pot would stop. One day this young man was going by her house and she was saying "Pot Boil." This fellow saw she had a good thing going. All he herd the lady say was "Pot Boil." He did not hear her say, "Pot stop." Now I want all of you kids to lift your hand if you have forgotten "N-the Grass" still trapped in the basket, and Willy is now selling Bean Soup. I'll get back to N-the Grass in a minute. The young man took the magic pot to his house and he said, "Pot Boil." He didn't know how to stop the Magic Pot. It just wouldn't stop. Soup was coming out of his doors, windows and flowing down the street. Now, as you mite remember, N-the Grass was about to leave his wicker basket like he was souped up. The lady came by my basket first and she said, "Basket Stop." The Magic Pot was nearby, and they both stopped at the same time. This goes to show you not to put all yore soup in the same Pot.

Oh, I'm not finished with N-the Grass, He crawled out of that basket with all that yeast and other stuff, and got a ticket. I got him out of all that trouble; and I told N-the Grass, I would git him a thick tablet to write his mem-wors on while I was playing the next time. I really tried hard to get better on my flute. Here I go again. I played fur airs again and still no snake. I opened the lid and there was a big sheet of paper from that tablet laying there saying he or she would play his part of the act if I would learn to play the flute better. I only played for a few Airs. You would think the least he or she could do would be to leave the tablet. I bought it for him or her. Well, I am still playin my flute. As you notice, I can't tell if N-the Grass is male or female. I can't see whether that really matters. One thing I have seen get better is He or She finally bought a set of ear plugs – which has really helped. I can't hardly afford to get me a pair. They don't pay a lot to see a Snake Charmer. If anyone sees anything wrong, tell me. I don't need the ear plugs too bad. I can take a lot of punishment. *Willy the Clown 10-4-2016*

I was so happy when I got up this morning! Well… that didn't last long; Puff, or an Ox got off in the ditch. To me, it was a very deep ditch; then, I was washing clothes and the spin cycle went out. I keep a spare Washer & Dryer in the barn. I'm glad it's nice weather. I thought I was too old to be working 23 Airs-A-Day. In the Army we got a half day off if we passed away. Here with Rocky and Puff I hardly get 5 minutes.

You can tell when I'm taking a break. We got the old washer out of the house and ventured out to the barn to get the 'Washer In Waiting'. Now I've been around awhile; as I opened the barn door Rocky said, "Uncle Bill, What is that?"

I said, "Rocky, that is what you call a 'Rub-Board".

Puff says, "It looks like it's been "In Waiting" a really long time. *Uncle Bill, Rocky, & Puff Neel.*

"Orkansaw Anglish"

Earn – Something that holds ashes.
En-tire – Where you usually find a nail.

All "Orkinsaw Anglish" words by Bill Neel

Chapter Seventeen
Willy the Clown – "Palm Reading" And "Fun on the Coast"

BN

{Palm Reading}

This was much better than listening to me play my flute, and trying to get my snake to get better or else. One problem I had – I didn't speak snake and he or she had no idea what I was saying. I think it had a lot to do with my spellin.

Ok – Let's get to Willy the Clown - "Palm Readin." I could read from one palm to fifty palms at the same time. Now you can see why Willy the Clown got the big Bucks. I would get a volen-tear from the audience. HA HA. I would tell the other kids to hold their hand out. No money, candy or other treats. Palm Readin is serious business. I would tell them to put one of their fingers in their hand and just follow along doing the same as I'm doing with the Volen-tear I have next to me. As we start, I put my finger on the Volen-tear's palm. I tell the audience to follow along with their finger on their hand and listen to what Willy the Clown is saying. If your finger gets all bent out of shape, don't worry about it. A hundred years from now, you won't remember it. I look in the audience, and 99% of the kids are really doing good with this project. I do this like all of Willy's stories. I butcher up different other little stories I have herd. After a good readin, I give all the kids a piece of real good candy. After the candy, I could change the hundred years to five minutes. I have as much fun doing this as the kids. Willy has not performed in several years. I really do miss doing this. Like I said before, I never had time to be stressed out.

Willy the Clown

Bill Neel

9-5-2016

"Fun on the Coast"

by *Willy the Clown*

I performed in several states. Probably my best was State of Shock. My mother was born in Mississippi. (Kos-es-ko) check spellin – I'll look. I did some work – or Fun should we say in Pass-a-goula, Mississippi. Let me spell it that way. I had a cute time with a young man with that werd. By Golly, I almost got run out of Mississippi when I was talkin' to him. I think his mother (almost sure) was about to get the roofing company and their hot tar and a chicken company to help her take care of me. When I put on a show, crazy things come to me and I tell everyone else. This time it got to be a serious piece of work I was doing. I felt like a crop duster about to run out of fuel. I'll bet you people are so excited to hear what happened.

Well, back then and even now, I like to watch and go to car races. Almost all or most of the young fellows had their little race tracks in their rooms; and really had a good time with them. I really enjoyed playing this game too. I didn't realize it would work into part of my act in Mississippi. Gosh, will I ever tell you what happened? Oh yes. I'll tell you in just a minute. I was talking with this young man and he was telling me all kinds of things. Maybe that is the reason I'm so smart. I've had a lot of good teachers. All of a sudden, I asked him - “what is a Goula?” We had just finished talking about race cars. I told him on my way to Mississippi, I had passed a car, pickup, 18 wheeler, motorcycle, and nearly passed out. I said I passed a Goula. I asked him if he could tell me what a Goula is. He really gits into this really serious. He is really trying real hard to explain what a Goula is. His mother is standing not too far away; and she gits more serious than her son. She starts telling me I'm poking fun at their town and the State of Mississippi. Well, I'm not like these people to git all upset over really nothing. I was having a good time and so was her son. I was not doing a TV News Show. These are some things you can really get serious about at times. I'm not perfect. If I was, I would ask for a lot more money than I'm getting. I also spend money in your area. No matter where I perform, I try to do a good job – so I mite be able to come back. I would never never say or do anything to hurt anyone's feelings. If I have, I'm sorry. This goes not only for Mississippi, but for all states which Willy the Clown has performed.

BN 9-5-2016

Chapter Eighteen
"Mall Tails"

"Tennessee Mall"
(It really got bad for the parent aparently)

This happened in a Tennessee Mall back in the mid-80's. This really happened too. I tried to change the subject real fast. Oh, I had an exciting job. Old age made me quit. Now back to the Mall. I did my little act for the kids, and when I finished, I always told the kids to throw Willy the Clown a kiss and I would throw one to them. I would spin around in circles, jump in the air, come down with my big shoes – making a big bang; then I would tell them to always mind their mom and dad. Well, I had been ending the show this way for a long time. I never had any trouble with the ending until now. There was this couple near me with 2 small boys. They seemed like a good, all together family. That looks real neat how I just said that about these folks. One of the little boys spoke up and said, "We are getting a Divorce from Daddy." Faces began to change a lot. They couldn't get out of there fast enough. I guess I should have started a "*Deer Willy* Will Listen." *BN*

P.S. I would be worse today than I am already. It pays to leave some things a-lone or loan??

BN *9-6-2016*

"Another <u>Tail</u> from a Mall in Tennessee"

(This almost got out of hand too or 2)

Willy the Clown can take care of most anything!

This was also in the mid 80's. I was real busy during this time. A lot of time the kids were in school and I would have fun with the adults and the younger children. After I look back on this (it's now 2016), I had a lot of fun with the adults too. A lot has changed since the 80's. If I was still doing *Willy the Clown* today, they would have the Swat Team and Bomb Squad chasing me. Let me explain what I just finished telling you. For a good while, I had done my <u>Man-uh-kin act</u>. I could stand perfectly still for long periods of time. A lot of the managers knew about this and they would stand back out of sight and watch all this crazy stuff. They were having a sidewalk sale. The manager would bring a small platform for me to STAND! He would put a sign on the clown suit, "Clearance $25.00. That was quite a bargain. The shoes were worth over $200.00. Then the price of the suit, wig, red nose and onion ring. Now, being in business for myself, I couldn't have too many Sails like this. With my makeup and white gloves, you couldn't tell if I was real or not. I would let a few people look this great bargain over. Then, this person came up and was checking the suit and everything and said, I think I'm going to buy this for my son. It was a lady – Not the lady I had seen before with the two boys. After a little bit, I said "Hi Hon." She started screaming and running down the mall, hollering all kinds of real, real bad words. I can't put those in this book. It was like - "The British are

Coming!" The reason I use this phrase a lot is I usta live in England, Arkansas. Soon as I got my second or third wind, I got back on the platform again. I just knew I had seen the last of that lady; and she didn't even buy my outfit. I had stood there for a long time; and that was my only customer. I look down the mall and here she comes with a friend. I could have known it was her if a million people were out there. She was still "Boiling" so to speak. Now I've been doing this for a good while and it's pretty hard for anyone to beet me at my own game. Well, you can't win every time. I did not move a muscle for a few seconds or maybe minutes. She was telling her friend how I had scared her, and her friend was looking and thought she had one too many to drink. She told that lady, "I am not Crazy and I'm going to show you he is real." I'm still not moving. She said, "Mr. Clown, my friend thinks I am crazy. If you don't move and let her know you are real, I'm going to step on your shoes." Ok,Ok, I had to do something now. She was no 90 pound week-ling. I started laughing and her friend said I was really good with my act. Everyone left happy and both went inside the store to the big Sail they were having. Oh, yes, I didn't have to leave to shine my shoes. I have Willy in Glitter on the toes of my shoes. It's hard to put glitter on them. I tell the kids to put their names on their shoes too.

This mall was about 300 miles from the other one.

Chapter Nineteen
"Old School and Babysitting a G.P.S."

(I'm Old, Old School – but I think you call it "G.P.S. – keeps you from getting lost?)

This has to do with Uncle Bill and Rocky the Wonder ~~Terrier~~ Dog. A few weeks ago, we were in the most Northern part of Arkansas. I hadn't driven in this area in over twenty years. Anyone could tell Rocky had never been in these parts. The way you can tell – if Rocky lays in his bed in the pickup, everything is ok. If he gits to an area he doesn't recognize, he is steady looking out of the window. In case I'm going to dump him, he will know his way back home. It's kinda like the little boy and girl and the old witch on that little weather vane that usta be real popular.

Now to the G.P.S. Part. Now, I don't use nothing but R.R.T. I keep teelin' you I'm old school. That means "Rocky Road Tellin." Rocky and I don't agree sometimes. I have to give in sometimes when I don't see cars, road signs or people. Rocky just sets there and bides his time until I finally turn around and go back where I started (and also need gasoline). You can see, I don't give up easy. You would think I would pay attention to R.R.T. By now. I'll never learn. What would I have to write about? I was trying to get to this small town, and all I could see was curves for miles and miles. I finally saw a little mom and pop grocery. No help here. It looked like it had been closed since the covered wagon days; and they all went West to look for Gold. I'm not blaming the highway department. They kept the highway in good

shape. I guess a few curves are good for everyone. I finally got on the right highway and still a lot of curves. Then I see a sign that said "This road is steep and a lot of curves." Now, what would have happened if I had a G.P.S. (Just a little funny). It would have said, "Could you stop your pickup? I feel dizzy and car sick. I don't want to make a mess." Like I will try to do the right thing for man or beast. I let the G.P.S. Out. After a few minutes, I said, "Rocky and I have a fur piece to go; and don't have time to set out here and Baby Sit a Machine."
It said, "Give me a little mower time. Act like you're picking up aluminum cans. Nobody will think you are a nut case that way." I told Rocky to git in the pickup. After Rocky got threw, I think he give the G.P.S. A short circuit. G.P.S. said, "If you want to be that way, we can throw rocks at each other." We saw a tractor coming with a great big mower. G.P.S. thought he was there to help throw rocks for her. We got out of there pretty quick. That mower was not on anyone's side. It was throwing rocks at everyone. I'm sure someday, after recycling, it will be a G.P.S. Again.

Don't you just love happy endings?

Rocky and *Uncle Bill*

(This Is For Real)

It sounds like something I made up.

** First Clinton, Arkansas Post Office **

I was looking at a cute ad from the past – like 1833.
(183 years ago). Back then, you didn't want to rob the Pony Express or Stage Coaches. You could make money honest by being a mail carrier if you had a good horse.

"An official United States Post Office has been established in Clinton, Arkansas. Daily mail service to Plummerville and Marshall Arkansas has been instituted. Weekly mail service has been scheduled to Searcy, Arkansas, Shiloh, Mountain View and Lewisburg, Arkansas.

Applications for Mail Carriers are now being taken at the Clinton, Ark. Post Office. All applicants must furnish their own horses."

You people today think about this. This kept beans, taters, and turnip greens on the table. They didn't start out being the "Post Master General."

Again

Land of Opportunity

Bill Neel *9-08-2016*

Chapter Twenty

"Orkinsaw Anglish"

{Bill Neel's Orkinsaw Anglish Dictionary}

Here's a small sample

I have started my "Orkinsaw Anglish Dictionary several times since the 1980's. I began the dictionary when I started my words in the England Democrat Paper – England, Ark. If you live around the Loanoke area, I don't see how you can live without it. Who else would know "The British Are Coming!" except the people who live in England. *BN*

Oh yes - "Land of Opportunity." Also, if you happen to move away, tell Jerry. I know for a fact, he can get the paper to you. I live in one county and I get my mail in another county. In all these years, I have never ever missed my paper.

Before I close this part, if any of you folks out there have any trouble with these words, Rocky (my Boston Terrier) can help you. I have been talking to him this way for several years. If he can't help you, just go on to the next word.

"This book is just for laughs. Don't take it serious. It does help some."

Bill Neel 8-28-2016

For your enjoymint, Here's a small sample of:

Bill Neel's Orkinsaw Anglish Dictionary.

(I hope you enjoy it – Learn something new every day!)

"A" - What you say when you have that big horn to your ear.

Abacus – Someone who talks real bad behind your back.

Abandon – When a band quits playing.

Abase – What you steal at a ball game when you can't find anything else. – also check "cleptoe".

Abate – Something you must take fishing.
Also check "debate" – to catch more fish!

Abode – What you use to build a house.

Acclaim – What you stake before anyone gits there.

Appeal – What you do before you eat yore apple.

"B" – A pretty good grade in school, or a real stinger.

Ball room – Where you go to play pool.

Bat-tree – What helps you start yore car.

Bed roll – What happens when you put your sleeping bag too close to a clift.

Bed-sore – When your bed gits mad at you.

Bi-son – What you do when you have all girls.

Blue moon – Read Uncle Bill's adventure

"Mower & Mower

Join Uncle Bill's on-going adventures in his next book. Also -- Be sure to keep a close lookout for the complete "Orkinsaw Anglish Dictionary" with more term-in-olo-gees than you can shake a stick at. All stories and wirds by: *Bill Neel* *11-15-16*

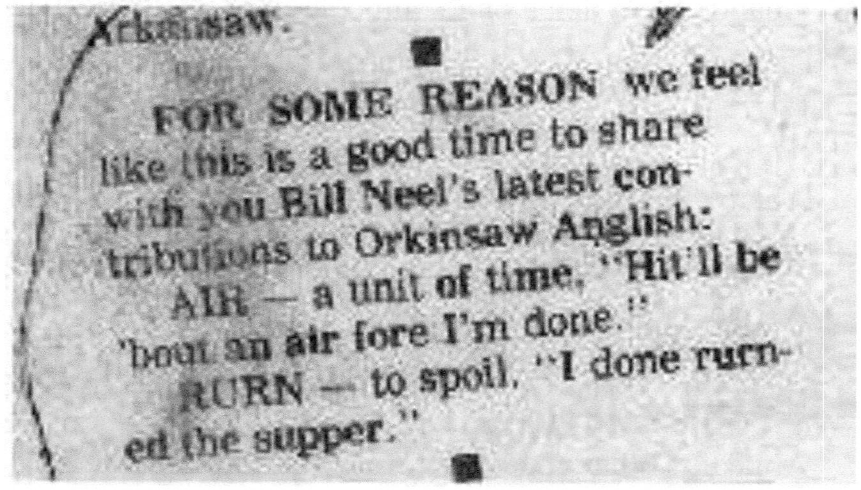

Orkinsaw.

FOR SOME REASON we feel like this is a good time to share with you Bill Neel's latest contributions to Orkinsaw Anglish:

AIR — a unit of time. "Hit'll be 'bout an air fore I'm done."

RURN — to spoil. "I done rurned the supper."

Above is a sample of Bill Neel's "Orkinsaw Anglish" as was often found in the England Democrat Newspaper!

THE END

?

Picture One

Picture Two

Picture Tree